Chicano-Mexicano Relations

Edited by
Tatcho Mindiola, Jr. and Max Martinez

Mexican American Studies Monograph No. 4
Mexican American Studies Program
University of Houston—University Park

CONTENTS

Introduction To
CHICANO-MEXICANO RELATIONS

Tatcho Mindiola, Jr. and Max Martinez

Chicano-Mexicano relations become the subject of scholarly attention at that point in the development of Chicanos when those relations are no longer possible to avoid. In the past two decades, Chicanos have increasingly become the subject of research studies in the social sciences. Much of this attention is due to the increasing presence of Chicanos in the university and in research centers. It would appear inevitable, then, that Chicanos would appropriate the subject of Mexico, the presence of Mexican immigrants in the U.S., and more importantly, the interrelationships among Chicanos and Mexicanos as principle areas of academic and intellectual concern. It is at this point that it is no longer possible to avoid Chicanos in the context of U.S.-Mexico relations.

How Chicano-Mexicano relations begin, the purpose to which they were at first devoted, and their contemporary trajectory form the substance of the essays here. It should be noted, however, that these essays represent initial efforts in what is virtually *terra incognita*. We are far from a comprehensive body of literature on the subject. Nevertheless, as this collection will amply attest, the structural framework for the disciplined study and research in Chicano-Mexicano relations is contained in the body of this volume.

This volume further is unique in that the present essays are the work of scholars who have actively participated in the development of this phase of Chicano-Mexicano relations. They were instrumental in providing the linkages necessary to establish the formal and informal relations between political and governmental leaders in Mexico and leaders in the Chicano community. Their experiences are recollected here in the form of scholarly discussion. Their contributions as participants inform their perspectives in an uncommon way, providing a unique dimension to the subject. Their observations are intimate, redolent with the special insight of someone who was there. At the same time, the detailed evidence is presented within the context of academic disciplines.

The history of Chicanos in the U.S. can be characterized as one of dispossesion, discrimination and subordination. In large measure this accounts for the absolute exclusion of Chicanos as a variable by scholars who specialize in U.S.-Mexico relations. In the extant books and articles on the topic Chicanos are not

1

mentioned at all. It is generally stipulated that ethnic groups in general are not important factors in foreign policy analysis. In this regard Chicanos would be no different from any other ethnic group. In practice, however, the stipulation does not hold if we consider the influential role played by Jews, Cubans, and now Blacks in the foreign policy of the United States toward Israel, Cuba and South Africa, respectively. In our judgment Chicanos have lacked the political and economic resources necessary to make significant inroad toward improving our standard of living much less influence U.S.-Mexico relations.

This, however, may be changing. In the last twenty five years, Chicanos have made gains in the areas of education, economics, and politics. Moreover, we have asserted ourselves as an important voice in the U.S. This assertiveness includes a demonstrable awareness of our ties to Mexico and a recognition that the U.S. and Mexico are involved in a relationship which for the most part is favorable to the U.S. Yet, despite the growing importance and measurable influence of the Chicano community and our increased awareness of Mexico, we nonetheless continue to remain on the periphery of scholarship concerning U.S.-Mexico relations.

If the scholarly community has ignored the Chicano variable in U.S.-Mexico relations, the U.S. government has not. If scholars have been unable to ferret out a direct relationship between Chicanos and Mexicanos in their intellectual deliberations, U.S. government officials have been keenly aware of it. Documents obtained through the Freedom of Information Act reveal that there is a considerable history of various U.S. intelligence gathering agencies maintaining numerous Chicano organizations and activities under surveillance.[1] Ostensibly, as a matter of national security, Chicanos were kept under surveillance for purposes of determining national loyalty. To whom do Chicanos pledge allegiance? To Mexico or to the United States? Does Mexico, as a foreign power, derive intelligence-gathering benefits from its citizens unlawfully residing in the U.S., or from naturalized former citizens or from the descendents of its citizens? A concommittant of the question of loyalty is the degree of potential subversiveness existing in the Chicano community. At various junctures in its history, questions of loyalty have preoccupied U.S. officials.

Certainly, the most infamous example of U.S. government policy toward an ethnic group whose loyalty is in question is the internment of Japanese-Americans during Second World War. During the First World War, similar suspicions arose concerning Chicanos. Chicanos then were suspected of being sympathetic toward Germany's attempt to recruit Mexico as an ally. The proximity of Mexico to the U.S. and the large number of Mexicans and Chicanos along the border areas fueled an already volatile situation. Since little research exists on the topic, we may conjecture that U.S. officials simply assumed that the Chicano community owed its loyalty and allegiance to Mexico. In other words, government policy failed to distinguish between Mexican citizens and American citizens of Mexican descent.

The muddled perspective of Chicanos by North Americans in general and those in government in particular is an important factor in U.S.-Mexico relations. There is, of course, no denying that there are many areas of affinity between Chicanos and Mexicanos, especially in regards to history, culture, family and residential proximity. The history of Chicanos, for example, begins in Mexico. It is difficult to understand the Chicano experience in the U.S. without beginning with the history of Mexico and the intersection of U.S. and Mexican history in the Southwest. It necessary to note that in the first half of the 19th century, the United

States appropriated nearly one third of all Mexican territory. In the aftermath of U.S. expansionism, an entire Mexicano society became U.S. citizens by default. Gradually, but certainly by the end of the 19th century, the Chicano lost virtually all of his social and economic influence. In sum, the Chicano population became subordinated. This status was confirmed by the perception of Chicanos as inherently lazy and lacking in ambition.

The process resulting in Chicano subordination has been largely accepted as a *priori* social condition by most scholars. Recently, however, Chicano scholars like Romo, Acuna, Camarillo and Griswold del Castillo have begun to analyze the historical process by which the subordinate status of Chicanos in the U.S. became institutionalized.[2] In so doing, they illuminate a critical aspect of Chicano studies; that is, the system into which people from Mexico emigrate.

Chicanos and Mexicanos are also of the same historical and cultural cloth. The key cultural link between us is language. Mexico is the largest Spanish-speaking country in the world. Spanish is the second most widely spoken language in the U.S. An estimated fifteen million people in the U.S. speak Spanish and this estimate would be larger if the number of immigrants in the U.S. without authorization could be accurately counted. The Spanish language then represents a cultural bond continually reinforced by Chicano and Mexicano interaction.

Family ties constitute another important factor in Chicano-Mexicano relations. Approximately 25 percent of all U.S.-born Mexicans have one or both parents who were born in Mexico.[3] Clearly, any analysis of Chicano-Mexicano relations would require that these ties be taken into consideration. Blood ties, then, are key to determining how Chicanos and Mexicanos perceive each other. Moreover, they are an important determinant of attitudes towards Mexico and the U.S.

Upon entry into the U.S., most Mexican immigrants settle in Chicano barrios. It is in these neighborhoods where most of the interaction between Chicanos and Mexicanos occurs. This is especially true along the U.S.-Mexico border in cities such as, Brownsville, El Paso, and San Diego. It also occurs in the large urban centers of the Southwest and Midwest such as Los Angeles, Houston, Chicago, and Detroit. Chicano barrios provide a natural environment for people from Mexico. The barrios constitute established kinship communities composed of settled immigrants and Chicanos. The kinship which informs the barrio reduces the newly-arrived immigrant's exposure to the Anglo world. It is far easier for immigrants to "blend" into the barrios where they may freely gather information about employment and housing. It is here, too, where they may be schooled in how American society functions. This latter is especially important to the recent immigrants.

While it is true that Chicanos and Mexicanos share certain affinities, there are significant differences between the two. The natural ties between Chicanos and Mexicanos are not absolute. For example, the Spanish spoken by Chicanos incorporates many linguistic features not found in the Spanish spoken by the newly-arrived immigrants. Thus, Spanish becomes as much an object of ridicule as a communications link. Further, Chicano culture is a syncretic culture and as much influenced by Anglo American culture as it is by Mexican culture. At the point of Chicano-Mexicano interaction in the barrio, there are varying degrees of discongruence and tension caused by cultural dissimilarities. Upon first exposure to Chicanos, Mexicanos react to Chicanos as people who have lost their culture and often refer to us, derogatorily, as "pochos."

3

The Mexican reaction to Chicanos illustrates an internal conflict prevalent among Chicanos, particularly among those with one or both parents born in Mexico. They tend to experience value conflicts as they must integrate what they learn at home from their parents and what they learn in the American school system. The result, in some instances, is a social distance between Chicanos and their Mexican-born parents relative to the manner in which the schools succeed in culturally assimilating Chicanos. Further, this same social distance is evident with respect to Mexican immigrants who reside in Chicano barrios. There is evidence indicating that within the barrios Mexicanos are residentially segregated from Chicanos. In San Antonio, for example, Valdez has found that within the barrios there are blocks and streets in which the housing is occupied exclusively by Mexicanos.[4] This tends to restrict the degree of interaction between the two groups and to heighten the degree of conflict between some segments of the Chicano population and Mexican immigrants.

The attitudes and perceptions of Chicanos toward Mexico and Mexicanos, and vice versa, is an empirical question calling for continued research and investigation. As Chicanos make more pronounced strides in determining our social and economic position in the U.S., there are a number of important policy items to consider in formulating the Chicano agenda. Among them will surely be Chicano-Mexicano relations and how it fits into the broader issue of U.S.-Mexico relations.

As stated earlier, many of the contributors to this volume actively participated in the development of the current phase of Chicano-Mexicano relations. Among those who made an initial, decisive gesture toward establishing those relations was Dr. Jorge Bustamante, who currently is the Director of El Centro Estudios Fronterizos in Tijuana, Mexico. Bustamante earned a law degree from the National University of Mexico in 1965. He continued his studies, earning a Ph.D. in Sociology from the University of Notre Dame.

Bustamante studied at Notre Dame during the heyday of the Chicano Movement and became acquainted with many of its leaders. He thus observed firsthand many of the events of the 1960s and 70s and as a result became thoroughly familiar with the subject of Chicanos. At the same time, Bustamante conducted research about the undocumented immigrant. For his dissertation, Bustamante posed as an undocumented immigrant and crossed into the U.S. illegally. His plan included being captured so he could gather information on how undocumented immigrants are treated once they are apprehended. His experiences are detailed in *Los Mojados* by Julian Zamora.[5] Zamora is one of the first Chicano scholars to address the issue of undocumented immigrants from Mexico.

Jorge Bustamante is now considered Mexico's leading authority on Mexican immigration to the U.S. He is also Mexico's leading expert on Chicanos. Bustamante has written extensively on the subject of Chicanos and he has lectured throughout Mexico on the subject. More importantly, he has begun to train a new generation of Mexican scholars whose areas of academic interest include Chicanos.

As the essays in this volume make clear, Bustamante has been the key figure in Mexico in fostering contacts between Chicanos and Mexican academic and political leaders. Jorge Bustamante, then, was instrumental in the development of Chicano-Mexicano relations as they exist today. His research and involvement in the subject continues unabated as issues critical to Chicanos and Mexicanos emanate from U.S.-Mexico relations.

Jose Angel Gutierrez is best known as the founder of the Raza Unida Party in Texas. He holds a Ph.D. in Political Science from the University of Texas at Austin and currently serves as the Commissioner on Hispanic Affairs for the State of Oregon.

Jose Angel Gutierrez has become a symbol of the militancy of Chicano college students in the 1960s and 70s. This militancy is variously known as the Chicano Movement. Self-determination was chief among the ideological underpinnings of the Chicano Movement. The formation of a Chicano-dominated and controlled political party implemented the concept of self-determination in a way hitherto unknown in the Chicano community.

Not surprisingly, the Raza Unida Party's most dramatic and significant successes occurred in Gutierrez' home in Zavala County, Texas. Beginning with the issue of equal educational opportunity in the school district, Gutierrez and the Raza Unida Party leadership created a model for organizing the putatively unorganizable migrant Chicano workers in rural areas. The success in Crystal City and Zavala County was soon duplicated in other rural communities in South Texas.

Ironically, or perhaps inevitably, as the Raza Unida Party became a factor to be reckoned with in Texas politics, government and foundation support for many of the Party's non-political projects began to wane. As these difficulties became more pronounced, Gutierrez turned to Mexico as a source of support. This coincided with Jorge Bustamante's efforts to arrange meetings between Mexico's then-President, Luis Echeverria, and Chicano leaders.

Bustamante appealed to Gutierrez for assistance in arranging those initial meetings. And thus, Jose Angel Gutierrez became the key Chicano figure in establishing the contact with Mexican academic and political leaders. The support Gutierrez sought was indeed forthcoming and, more importantly, as the exchanges continued and were expanded to include more issues, Gutierrez became one of the key advocates of more involvement on the part of Chicanos in issues involving Mexico.

Rodolfo O. de la Garza is currently serving as a special assistant to the Chancellor of the University of Texas system. He has a Ph.D. in Political Science from the University of Arizona. De la Garza is representative of the Chicano academic who has embraced U.S.-Mexico relations as one of his areas of intellectual concern, with particular emphasis on whether or not Chicanos can be influential in the area.

Professor de la Garza is the first to consider the role of Chicanos in the United States foreign policy towards Mexico. In several articles, de la Garza examines the possibility of Chicanos becoming an influential factor in U.S. foreign policy. He further develops a theoretical model which specifies various Chicano interest groups and determines their potential for influencing how the U.S. will act towards Mexico.[6]

Interestingly, de la Garza concludes that Chicanos are not yet a significant factor in U.S.-Mexico relations, a posture which some consider conservative. Nevertheless, his articles reflect original analysis, and they also serve to keep advocates of such a relationship more realistically attuned to the social, economic and political power of Chicanos and their potential for influencing U.S.-Mexico relations.

Armando Gutierrez has a Ph.D. in Political Science from the University of Texas at Austin. He currently serves as a policy advisor to the Rainbow Coalition in Washington, D.C. Gutierrez also served as an advisor in the candidacy of the Reverend Jesse Jackson for the presidency of the United States. During his years as a student and later as an academic, Gutierrez was a close associate of both Jorge

Bustamante and Jose Angel Gutierrez. Armando Gutierrez has participated in virtually all of the meetings between the past three Presidents of Mexico and Chicano leaders. He was instrumental in obtaining and administering the Becas para Aztlan and the Summer Becas programs, both funded by the government of Mexico and both resulting from leadership exchanges between Mexico and Chicanos. Both Beca programs were designed exclusively for Chicanos.

Armando Gutierrez went on to become the chief Chicano contact with Jorge Bustamante. During the presidential campaign of Miguel de la Madrid, Gutierrez served as de la Madrid's advisor on Chicano affairs. He has written several position papers on Chicanos for various political and academic leaders in Mexico and was considered for the position of Chicano advocate within the Mexican government. The idea was discussed but never implemented by the de la Madrid administration. Armando Gutierrez, then, represents the Chicano activist-scholar who believes that Chicanos are destined to play a significant part in influencing, if not indeed, determining the politics of the U.S. government toward Mexico.

Gilberto Cardenas has a Ph.D. in Sociology from the University of Notre Dame and is an Associate Professor of Sociology at the University of Texas at Austin. Cardenas and Jorge Bustamante studied together at Notre Dame. Both studied under Julian Zamora. Cardenas was one of the first Chicano scholars to focus on Mexican immigrants from a historical as well as a sociological point of view. Cardenas, as well, is one of the Chicano scholars who have come to the defense of undocumented immigrants through empirically-based research. Generally, Cardenas' research shows that Mexican immigrants have been and continue to be a positive force for the U.S. economy and for Chicanos in particular, since many of the immigrants settle in Chicano barrios and become involved in the barrio or ethnic economy.[7] The relationship between Chicanos and Mexicanos via the ethnic community is Cardenas' most recent area of investigation.

Nestor Rodriguez is an Assistant Professor of Sociology at the University of Houston, University Park Campus. He holds a Ph.D. in Sociology from the University of Texas at Austin. Rodriguez's concern is the relationship between Mexicanos and Chicanos in the workplace. His research reminds us that interaction between both groups occurs within the parameters of institutional as well as non-institutional settings. Within institutional settings, such as the workplace, the relationship is determined by the needs of the employers as well as the internal workings of each group.

In summary, the scholars whose essays are presented in this monograph are the first to focus on the relationship between Chicanos and Mexicanos, members of the same ethnic group who share similarities as well as differences resulting from history and geographical changes. It is our prediction that the area of Chicano-Mexicano relations will continue to grow and that Chicano and Mexicano scholars will play the dominant and leading role in defining areas of concern. This monograph is a first step in that direction.

FOOTNOTES

1. Jose Angel Gutierrez, "Chicanos and Mexicanos Under Surveillance: 1940 to 1980," unpublished paper.
2. Ricardo Romo, *East Los Angeles*, University of Texas Press, Austin, Texas 1983. Rodolfo Acuna, *Occupied America*, Harper and Row, New York, 1981. Alberto Camarillo, *Chicanos in a Changing Society: From Mexican Pueblos to American Barrios in Santa Barbara and Southern California 1848-1930*, Harvard University Press, Cambridge, 1979. Richard Griswold del Castillo, *The Los Angeles Barrio 1850-1890*. University of California Press, Los Angeles, 1979.
3. Current Population Reports, "Ancestry and Language in the United States," November 1979, Series P-23, No. 116, U.S. Census Bureau, Washington D.C.
4. Avelardo Valdez, "Residential Patterns of Chicanos, Undocumented Mexicans and Anglos in San Antonio (Bexar County), Texas: An Assessment of Recent Changes and Social Costs," in Harley L. Browning and Rodolfo O. de la Garza (eds.) *Mexican Immigrants and the Mexican Americans: An Evolving Relation*, Center for Mexican American Studies, University of Texas at Austin, 1986.
5. Julian Zamora, *Los Mojados*, University of Notre Dame Press, Notre Dame, Indiana, 1971, Chapter 7.
6. Rodolfo O. de la Garza, "Chicano-Mexicano Relations: A Framework for Research," *Social Science Quarterly*, March, 1982, Volume 63, No. 1.
7. Gilbert Cardenas and Estevan Flores, "Social, Economic and Demographic Characteristics of Undocumented Mexicans in the Houston Labor Market: A Preliminary Report," Department of Sociology, University of Texas, Austin.

CHICANO-MEXICANO RELATIONS: FROM PRACTICE TO THEORY*

Jorge A. Bustamante

INTRODUCTION

During the last decade in Mexico, there has been an appreciable increase of interest in Chicanos, their history and heterogeneity, their struggles and achievements. This interest and understanding represent phenomena of relatively recent origin. This interest, however, has not been sufficient to eliminate the stereotypical perceptions which shape the view of Chicanos held by many Mexicans. These stereotypes have not been formed in only one way. The ignorance which substitutes the stereotype for reality is shared by both, Mexicans and Chicanos.

Relations between Chicanos and Mexicans have diversified and have improved in spite of precarious levels of mutual information. At the close of the decade of the 60s, there were few general studies about the Chicano as an ethnic group; in Mexico, there was not a single study available in Spanish. Similarly, knowledge about Mexico among Chicanos was extremely limited, inasmuch as formal education programs included little about Mexico, other than distortions arising from ethnocentric or simply racist prejudices toward Mexico. The mass communications media of the United States covered Mexico only in times of natural disaster or spectacular crimes.

This increased intensity and diversification of relations between Chicanos and Mexicanos makes it necessary to formulate a conceptual framework, one which will permit an understanding based upon the identification and definition of the reality of the relations in practice.

This essay is divided into three parts. The first part will attempt a very general historical outline on which to base a contextual framework of relations between Chicanos and Mexicans. The second will be a conceptual focus on the distinct relations between Chicanos and Mexicans. This part will conclude with a section of the relations between the government of Mexico and Chicanos from the point of view of this author who personally witnessed events, activities, and situations occurring between 1972 and the present. The third part will address itself to a conceptual framework for these relations emphasizing research and the future development of relations between Chicanos and Mexicans.

*Translated from Spanish by Max Martinez

8

HISTORICAL ANTECEDENTS

Prior to 1970, relations between Chicanos and Mexicans may be characterized as existing on the personal level. Systematic relations among organizations of both groups were non-existent. This is not to say that relations between organizations have not existed historically. On the contrary. The wave of migration from Mexico to the United States at the beginning of this century was instrumental in the rise of organizations which functioned as satellites of organizations headquartered in Mexico. Reciprocally, there were corresponding Chicano organizations in Mexico. Studies by a number of Chicano historians, notably Juan Gomez Quiñones, Rodolfo Acuna, Emilio Zamora, Luis Arroyo, and Victor Nelson Cisneros have documented the existence of relations between Chicanos and Mexicans in political, community, and union organizations during different periods in the first half of this century.[1]

Following World War II, there was a continual decrease in contact between organizations on both sides of the border to the point where they virtually disappeared in the 50s and 60s. An example of the virtual absence of understanding in Mexico of the situation of Chicanos in the United States is the case of Reies Lopez Tijerina and his struggles to recover lands taken away from Chicanos in New Mexico. His many journeys to Mexico to gain support for his effort culminated with his expulsion by the Mexican government acting on information supplied by the government of the United States.[2]

One reason for the use of the term, "Chicano" to refer to the population of Mexican origin in the United States, is the relationship which exists between the rise of the struggles of Chicanos in different parts of the United States toward the end of the decade of the 60s and the rise of a new stage in relations between Mexicans and descendents of Mexicans with United States citizenship. The struggles of the 60s can be situated in an historical constant which began practically with the military conquest of northern Mexico and which ended with the dismemberment of our national territory in 1848.

The visibility which the Chicano struggles acquired in the United States press in the 60s went under the rubric, "Chicano Movement." This visibility generated a false impression that Chicanos had no antecedents with the even more intense struggles before the 60s. Even though the term "Chicano" was not accepted as a self-identification by all citizens of Mexican origin in the United States, it was given wide spread visibility by the news media. For the purposes of this paper, it is important to emphasize that it was the struggles at the end of the 60s which mark the origin of a new chapter in the relations between Chicanos and Mexicans.

During this period, the press in the United States placed particular emphasis on the struggles led by Cesar Chavez. The fact that Cesar Chavez was the leader of farmworkers in California contributed to the perpetuation in Mexico of a stereotype that the struggles of Chicanos were mainly those of rural peasants. For a long time, this distorted the perception of Chicanos in Mexico. The intensive phenomenon of urbanization of the population of Mexican origin in the United States, which began early in this century, was unknown.

This phenomenon, as old as it is, explains the fact that more than 90% of the Chicano population is now urban. This explains as well the struggles rising in the 60s and which were characterized as the Chicano Movement were basically a movement in an urban context. Consequently, its major expressions were among university students and among community organizations in the barrios of large cities where the population of Mexican origin is concentrated.

One of the most notable results of these struggles was the institutionalization of Chicano Studies in the university. The formation of programs, centers, and departments of Chicano Studies at major universities not only legitimized the study of history and the problematic of this ethnic group, but it systematized historical research and it also generated scientific and artistic production. These endeavors initiated the build-up of an increasing body of knowledge of the heterogeneous reality of the Chicano. It was inevitable that under the systematic study of the historical presence of Chicanos in the United States their relationship with Mexico would surface. It became, then, a matter of rediscovery.

The search of Mexico by Chicanos was manifested initially through the influence of the great Mexican muralists and printmakers on Chicano art at the start of the 60s. Among other accomplishments, Chicanos appropriated much wallspace in the universities and in the barrios. On them, they recreated their struggles, their frustrations, their aspirations, and their myths under the influence of Diego Rivera, David Alfaro Siqueiros, and Jose Clemente Orozco. Chicano artists perceived a parallel between the great Mexican muralists and the revolutionary period in the first part of this century, and their struggle of the 60s. This creative representation in a proliferation of murals and posters signalled the acquisition of a self-identity and did not necessarily mean an objective reflection of their true reality.

Chicanos searched as well in Mexican literature. This rediscovery of Mexican literature was also the result of a process of recuperating the Spanish language. It occurred among those young people who, until 1971, were victims of legislation in force throughout the United States which prohibited speaking Spanish in the schools. An infraction of these laws was accompanied by the condemnation of Spanish as something dirty belonging to a past with which they had to break if they sought to achieve success in North American society. If Chicanos recovered their Spanish, freeing it of its stigma of subversiveness of inferiority, it was done in the face of an educational system designed to compel an assimilation dependent upon the effacement of the culture of origin.

Chicanos won the right to read Vasconcelos, whose notions of the Bronce Race (*raza de bronce*) and Cosmic Race (*raza cosmica*) produced a strange fascination among Chicano intellectuals who had been using the term, "la raza," colloquially in the way it has been used ancestrally in the north of Mexico to refer to "our people."[3] There was not a single Mexican intellectual, demonstrating his profound ignorance of the history of Chicanos, who did not identify the frequent use of the term, "la raza" with racial prejudice. The misunderstandings between Chicanos and Mexicans were sustained concomitantly with their increasing rediscovery of each other.

Octavio Paz' *Labyrinth of Solitude* became the archetype for what Chicanos perceived to be a typically elitist perspective among Mexicans.[4] Without understanding the historical context of the development of the struggles of the Chicano in the United States since 1848, these Mexicans were scandalized by the *pachucos* of the 1940s. They were left shocked upon hearing one Chicano say goodbye to another with, "ah te wacho, ese."

The introduction of English into Spanish was an act of linguistic perversion for some middle class Mexicans. It was condemned and labelled with the classist category, of "pochismo." However, for Chicanos, it was an act of loyalty to their language of origin and to their ethnic group, in spite of an educational system and a dominant culture in the United States committed to stripping them away.

The influence of English on Spanish occurred in the face of the impossibility of a legitimate teaching of Spanish grammar. The result was a linguistic phenomenon, translational in character, erupting from political, economic, social, and cultural conditions principally in the border regions. Nevertheless, this linguistic result, for many Mexicans, was the cause of horror and scorn; at the same time it was, for Chicanos, the cause of estrangement from Mexicans.

The Second World War produced assimilation without precedent among Chicanos. For the first time, they entered as an ethnic group into an institution which defined them as "Americans." This institution was the armed services of the United States. Despite the fact that some local officials in Texas refused burial in the Anglo cemeteries to Chicano heroes killed in action,[5] the process of assimilation accelerated at an unusual pace. Inasmuch as the generations following World War II were better prepared for the process of assimilation, the gap in communications between the Mexican middle class and Chicanos increased.

SOCIAL SECTORS IN THE RELATIONS BETWEEN CHICANOS AND MEXICANS

To understand the relation between Mexicans and Chicanos it is necessary to make a conceptual distinction—that of the social sectors of Chicanos and Mexicans. The constant migratory stream of Mexicans to the United States has produced and maintained contact between native-born Mexicans and Mexican descendents in the United States. Yet, Chicanos well can be defined as the descendents of Mexican immigrants, an immigrant Mexican laborer is not the same as a Chicano. They are distinguished by the following factors.

a) The temporary nature of the majority of Mexican migrants, tied to their work objectives in the United States, with a corresponding absence of a desire to return to the country of their ancestors. Migrant laborers, in general, look for better wages and better jobs which will permit them a better quality of life in their places of origin in Mexico. Chicanos, in general, seek access to and participation in the social, economic and political structures in the United States. They seek conditions of equality in the context of an ethnic and political pluralism. Their struggles as such are oriented to living better in the United States, but they wish to do so under the principle of maintaining their ethnic identity within that citizenship.

b) At an increasing level, Chicanos and Mexican immigrants may be distinguished by their different socio-economic levels. Generally, Chicanos have higher levels of economic existence than do Mexican immigrants. In their immediate relations in the United States, it is more probable to find Chicanos in supervisory positions and the Mexicans as workers and not the reverse.

c) Furthermore, they are distinguished by their national loyalties. Generally, the national loyalty of Mexican immigrants is to Mexico and that of Chicanos to the United States. This difference in national loyalties is independent of common cultural identifications.

In practice, cultural identifications co-exist and are not incompatible among Chicanos and Mexicans. On the other hand, there are the indifferences in their respective national loyalties. In this respect, Chicanos are not different from other

11

ethnic groups in the United States, in spite of the fact that Chicanos have been accused of being potential or actual "traitors to their country" because of the interest expressed in coming closer to Mexico. It is worth noting that those who have made this aberrant accusation do not extend it to other ethnic groups, for example the Jews when they wish closer ties with and offer political and economic support for Israel.

In speaking of communication between the social sectors of Chicanos and Mexicans in the United States, it may be said that the socio-economic distance between them was minimal for a long time. After World War II, the distance increased, bringing about certain consequences in the relations between the two groups. While the distance was at a minimal level, there was little necessity for an analytical distinction. Now, because of generational removal from Mexico and as-similation there is a significant distance, and it becomes necessary to take it into account.

The distance in socio-economic levels between both groups has not been concommitant with a decrease in cultural identification, nor is it correlated to the solidarity and support which, without exception, Chicano organizations have ex-pressed and practiced in favor of undocumented Mexican workers in recent years. At the personal level, Chicanos have had greater variations in their appreciation of Mexican immigration, more so than at the organizational level. Thus, the necessity to pinpoint the terms of the relationship.

To the extent that a significant relationship has been maintained between Mexican immigrants and Chicanos in the United States, the social sectors of the regions where Mexican emigration originates maintain a relation which may be characterized by family ties more so than by organizational character or from group to group. Among the families of migrants from Guanajuato, Jaliso, Michoa-can, Zacatecas, San Luis Potosi, Durango, or the remainder of northern Mexico, the world of the Chicano is not foreign, although it is not native. As in the past, when the "pachuco" style reached youth fashions in Mexican border cities from where we got German Valdez, the pachuco—now "Tin Tan;" now the "cholo" style, in dress as in manner of walking and writing on the walls of the barrios, has similarly penetrated and is evident beyond border cities into the interior. This is particularly so in those cities along the western route from the middle of Mexico to the United States.

In the social sectors of Mexican cities where emigration to the United States is more intense, the cultural distinction between Chicano and Mexican tends to dissipate without disappearing altogether. The relations between Chicanos and Mexicans in those cities is not intellectualized, as it is simply a lived family reality or a migrant experience.

To the extent that emigration to the United States is removed from certain sectors of Mexican society, there is a great distance between Mexicans and Chica-nos, as well as an increased lack of communication and the exchange of mutual information. It is in the urban sectors of the Mexican middle class and among Chicanos at the university level where a new stage in relations between Chicanos and Mexicans is gestating. Paradoxically, it is among these groups where there has been the greatest of misunderstandings. Higher levels of education among these groups are not necessarily associated to higher capabilities of mutual understand-ing. It appears as if the opposite would be the case.

Among the middle class sectors, relations between Chicanos and Mexicans have come about more at the organizational level and less at the individual level.

Mexicans of the middle class tend to know more about Chicano organizations and less about Chicano history or individuals. Still, there is developing in Mexico City an unusual phenomenon by the exhibition of the film, *Zoot Suit* by Luis Valdez.[6] Its title in Spanish has been translated to "Latin Fever." This musical film concerns a historical incident at Sleepy Lagoon in Los Angeles in 1942 in which racial prejudice against Chicanos surfaced. It was originally a success on the stage for several years in the late 1970's in Los Angeles. When it was presented on Broadway, it was a failure which caused its author to attempt to universalize the original theme with the object of capturing a large non-Chicano audience.

It seems that the film did not attract as many Anglos as the play did on Broadway. However, it did manage to captivate a middle class Mexican audience in Mexico City. Thus, the film has not only been a box-office success, it has also fixed the eye of the Mexican middle class on the individuality and artistic quality of Chicanos. It is greeted with applause in an atmosphere without precedent. It may be that *Zoot Suit* is provoking a cultural phenomenon of togetherness between Chicanos and the Mexican middle class which organizational efforts during past decades have been unable to achieve. This phenomenon contrasts with the noteworthy ignorance and indifference of middle class circles at the beginning of the seventies.

An example of that ignorance with respect to the significance of the world of the Chicano for Mexico was the resistance which a proposal by this writer to the Universidad Nacional Autonoma de Mexico met in 1972. It was an attempt to establish a course on Chicanos in the curricula of the School of Political and Social Sciences. The initial response conveyed the attitude that, "the question of Chicanos is a passing fad," and thus it did not justify the establishment of a formal course in the institution. It was finally accepted as a course under the title, "Sociology of Minorities: The Chicano." The first time the course was offered, eight students enrolled, of which the majority did so to fill out their class schedules according to times they had available and not because of any specific interest in the material.

In 1972, there was only one book in Spanish which analyzed, in a general and historical way, the situation of Chicanos in the United States. This was *North from Mexico* by Carey McWilliams.[7] It had only been a few months since the work had been translated from English and published by Fondo de Cultura Economica. Ten years later, upon completing a bibliographical compilation in the Border Studies Program of El Colegio de Mexico, this writer found three hundred titles of works in Spanish on Chicanos. This increase speaks eloquently of the increase of interest in Chicanos and of the sources of information available in Mexico. It should be noted that on the second occasion when the course, "Sociology of Minorities: The Chicano," was offered, one hundred twenty students enrolled, the majority of them because of serious interest in the subject.

In less than ten years, interest in Chicanos within university circles in Mexico City and the rest of Mexico has been reflected in the creation of courses on Chicanos. Similarly, it is reflected in the number of theses written for the bachelor's degree in any number of disciplines. Another factor which has contributed to this expansion of interest has been scholarship programs for Chicano students offered by the government of Mexico through the Consejo Nacional de Ciencia y Tecnologia (National Council on Science and Technology). The presence of Chicano students participating in these scholarship programs has contributed significantly to increase the amount of information and understanding on the part of many Mexicans from the middle social classes in a university context. Added to this should be the role of seminars, conferences, and academic events during the last few years in various universities in this country which have had the Chicano as a central theme. The very positive reception which these academic events have had during the past five years contrasts with the experience of "The First Seminar on Chicanos in Mexico," sponsored by the School of Political and Social Sciences at UNAM in November 1972. Two days before the beginning of the seminar there was a strike. Dr. Pablo Gonzalez Casanova unexpectedly resigned as President of the University and the event was cancelled. This decision was made after several of the invited Chicano participants had arrived in Mexico City. The invited Chicanos were unaware of the implications which Chairman Gonzalez Casanova's resignation might have had for university autonomy and were reluctant to participate in the seminar because of the strikes. The result was almost the opposite of what had been intended by the seminar. That is, the result caused a major division and mutual alienation between Chicanos and Mexicans instead of a step toward closer relations.

THE UNIONS

Relationships between Chicanos and Mexican union organizations during the last twenty years have been more sporadic than structured along permanent bases or institutionalization. The most noteworthy assemblies have taken place around the issue of undocumented Mexican workers in the United States. One factor which perhaps has made unity difficult is the traditional position of the AFL-CIO against immigration in general and Mexican immigration in particular. In the past, the AFL-CIO has supported proposals with restrictive measures or coercion against Mexican immigration. The alignment to the AFL-CIO position by the Farmworkers Union of Cesar Chavez contributed to the confusion with respect to relations between Chicano and Mexican union organizations.

Despite the fact that Cesar Chavez expressly modified his initial position favoring restrictions on Mexican immigration, there prevailed in Mexico the impression that the Chicano union movement continued its opposition to Mexican immigration to the United States. In recent years, there have been some sporadic meetings between union organizations with a majority Chicano membership and Mexican union organizations. They have produced declarations, more rhetorical than practical, with respect to human rights and labor rights of undocumented Mexican workers in the United States. This area of relations between Chicano and Mexicans has not been sufficiently studied to enable one to make a proper assessment. The majority of Chicanos belong to the working class and many may have the same transnational corporation as an employer; thus, the relation between Chicano and Mexican unionists is as precarious as it is sporadic.

ENTREPRENEURIAL SECTOR IN THE RELATIONS
BETWEEN CHICANOS AND MEXICANS

Albeit very few entrepreneurs of Mexican origin accept the term "Chicano" to identify themselves ethnically because of the connotation of political militancy, it is important to outline some salient aspects of the relations between entrepreneurs of Mexican origin in the United States and Mexican entrepreneurs. The existence of entrepreneurial organizations under the title, "Mexican American Chambers of

Commerce," has been conducive, in an organizational way, to establishing contact between entrepreneurs of Mexican origin and Mexican entrepreneurs.

In contrast to the relation between Chicano and Mexican union organizations, which decreased in intensity as the present century advanced, relations between Chicano and Mexican entrepreneurs is a relatively recent phenomenon. It is as recent as the appearance of significant numbers of Chicano entrepreneurs. It is not, however, a matter of a very generalized relation. Its existence, though inchoate, has emerged out of a growing awareness among Mexican entrepreneurs of what could be called an "ethnic" market with appetites and preferences determined by cultural traditions. This response on the part of consumers is beyond objective necessities or better quality in the products imported to the United States.

A growing number of Mexican entrepreneurs have discovered that Mexican cultural traditions produce a demand for culturally associated Mexican products on the part of consumers of Mexican origin. This awareness by Mexican entrepreneurs is not always extended to a search for co-participation with Chicano entrepreneurs. Many Mexican entrepreneurs, though aware of the existence of this ethnic market in the United States, are not aware of the entrepreneurial capacity existing among Chicanos. The comparative advantage of Chicanos and Mexicans have in entrepreneurial activity resulting from a commonality of language and cultural tradition has not been sufficiently developed by either Chicano or by Mexican entrepreneurs. Nevertheless, the possibility for increasing opportunities exists. This relation between Chicano and Mexican entrepreneurs is as much at the individual level as it is between organizations characteristic of the private sector in both countries.

THE GOVERNMENT OF MEXICO AND CHICANOS

In May of 1972, prior to a conference with President Richard Nixon scheduled for June of the same year, President Luis Echeverria scheduled consultation meetings with representatives from diverse sectors. One of the persons with whom President Echeverria spoke was Professor Gaston Garcia Cantu. On my return from the United States in 1972, following the completion of my doctoral studies at the University of Notre Dame, I had the opportunity to show my thesis to Professor Garcia Cantu. He became very interested in the results of my research on the subject of undocumented Mexican migration to the United States. Upon his interview with President Echeverria, Professor Garcia Cantu referred him to the problem of the migration of Mexican workers to the United States and to the research I had conducted on the subject. President Echeverria then asked Professor Garcia Cantu to invite me to a conversation with him.

A part of the report which I gave to President Echeverria was a reference to the role of Chicano organizations in the protection of undocumented Mexican workers in the United States. President Echeverria became very interested in the subject of Chicanos. He asked me to arrange a meeting for him during his visit to the United States so as to express his gratitude to Chicanos as President of Mexico for the solidarity offered to Mexican citizens in the United States in search of work. I then invited Gilbert Cardenas (now an Associate Professor at U.T. Austin) to join me in a team work to negotiate meetings with some Chicano leaders and intellectuals. We were not sure at the time, that our personal motives for doing this were understood. Most people thought we were Mexican government agents which we were not. We attempted to facilitate communication process congruent with our

15

personal views about Chicano-Mexicano relations. Finally, President Echeverria met with several groups. He was particularly impressed with the group led by Jose Angel Gutierrez in Crystal City, Texas. At the time, Dr. Gutierrez was National Chairman of the La Raza Unida Party.

After demonstrating great interest in the manner in which La Raza Unida Party had obtained local power through the electoral process, President Echeverria gladly accepted the proposal from Dr. Gutierrez that the government of Mexico fund a scholarship program for Chicanos in Mexican universities. In the meeting between President Echeverria and the group from Crystal City, the basis for a personal relationship between the President and the Chicano leader was established.

This personal relationship brought forth various programs for Chicanos supported by the government of Mexico. Among the most notable was a program for the distribution of Mexican books to libraries. The books concentrated on Mexican history and followed a distribution criteria suggested by Dr. Gutierrez; a program of tours by groups of Mexican artists to various cities in the United States where large Chicano populations were concentrated; a program of touring exhibits of paintings and prints by Mexican artists; a program of conferences with Chicanos and Mexican intellectuals; a plan to finance a motion picture directed by a Chicano filmmaker with a subject matter centered on relations between Mexicans and Chicanos; a scholarship program for Chicano students with an emphasis on training medical doctors who would serve in clinics in Chicano communities throughout the southwestern United States.

The personal preference by President Echeverria for the leader, Jose Angel Gutierrez, aroused jealousies among members of other Chicano organizations in the United States. They impugned the representatives of Dr. Gutierrez as a spokesman for all Chicano groups in the United States before the government of Mexico.

The Chicano Movement at the end of the 60s and the beginning of the 70s produced a charismatic leadership phenomenon manifested by the predominance of four leaders of national prominence who represented four different experiences, strategies, and organizational objectives. These four leaders were: Cesar Chavez in California, Rodolfo "Corky" Gonzalez in Colorado, Reies Lopez Tijerina in New Mexico, and Jose Angel Gutierrez in Texas. President Echeverria tried to establish communications with all four. He managed only to develop a relationship with Jose Angel Gutierrez which resulted in concrete activity and, second, with Reies Lopez Tijerina.

Although President Echeverria tried to pass on his preference for these four leaders to President Lopez Portillo, the evolution of the Chicano Movement, so characteristic of its heterogeneity, surpassed the powerbase of the four previously mentioned leaders. The development of new leadership drastically modified the Chicano Movement. It gave rise to some, who perhaps, were less in touch with community bases but who were better connected to the traditional structures of mobility within the context of United States politics. During his presidency, Lopez Portillo preferred a new type of Chicano leader, one better suited to the political process of training public officials or representatives of legitimate organizations supported by foundations of national importance. The process displayed a preference for the recruitment of business executives or specialists technicians than militants mobilizing the masses.

Neither President Echeverria nor President Lopez Portillo sought to obtain political gain through their relations with representatives of Chicano organizations.

However, during the presidency of Lopez Portillo, a few Chicano spokesmen began to collectively substitute the personal relationship between Chicano leaders and the President of Mexico. They began to circulate the idea of developing a Chicano lobby to look for support from the Mexican government.

Although the idea was never expressly supported by a Mexican functionary in high position, it was put forward as if it were an objective in the relations between the government of Mexico and Chicanos. The idea was further fueled by various leaders of Chicano organizations who found a way to obtain visibility in the mass communications media of the United States. Through an audience with the President of Mexico, they received the attention of correspondents from some major United States newspapers and magazines. The visit of the leaders to Los Pinos in Mexico City was converted into an avenue of access to the major presses of the United States. This access would have been less probably for the frequent visitors of the various government offices in Mexico. This practice among some Chicano leaders, in addition to a few statements by President Lopez Portillo—one in particular made at the Zocalo in Mexico City after his return from the United States and a visit with President Carter—produced a false politicization of the relationship between the government of Mexico and Chicanos. This politicization was false because it did not come from any political objective on the part of the President of Mexico. It was false moreover because it did not stem from the concrete possibility of political influence by Chicano representatives at the national level in the United States. However, in the eyes of many observers, the relationship did acquire the appearance of a quest for political objectives.

If some scholarship programs, offered as an expression of unity in the administration of President Echeverria, did become institutionalized, the relationship of the government of Mexico with Chicanos was much less diversified, much less defined, much less organized, and must less productive from what it had been in the previous administration. By the time of the electoral campaign of Miguel de la Madrid, the number of Chicano organizations interested in establishing relationships with the candidate of the Partido Revolucionario Institucional (PRI) had multiplied to an extraordinary level.

During the campaign for the Presidency of Mexico, Miguel de la Madrid proposed a new model for the relationship based on two principles: the circumscription of the relationship between the government of Mexico and Chicano representatives to an exclusive area of cultural relations. It would have as its purpose the diffusion and reinforcement of the history and culture of Mexico in Chicano communities in the United States. The other principle was a search for the institutionalization of relations between the government of Mexico and Chicanos in the cultural arena, as previously outlined.

If the idea of institutionalizing relations between the government of Mexico and Chicanos has not yet become a reality, it is clear that President de la Madrid does not wish the relationship between his government and Chicanos to have a political character in the least. It is to remain at a level circumscribed by the mutual reinforcement of cultural ties between the people of Mexico and Chicanos.

TOWARD A CONCEPTUAL FRAMEWORK FOR RELATIONS BETWEEN CHICANOS AND MEXICANS

In speaking of relations between Mexicans and Chicanos, the sectors of each society which looks for or enters into the relations, on either side of the border, ought to always be distinguished. There could be serious mistakes made if the tone and orientation of the relation were generalized in order to involve all of Mexico or all Chicanos. As for Chicanos, their relationship to Mexico ought to stem from the principle that their interest in Mexico is completely compatible with their loyalty to the national symbols and institutions of the United States. The practice of relations between Chicanos and Mexicans demonstrated that compatibility is indubitably feasible. The supposition of incompatibility between an interest in Mexico on the part of Chicanos and their national loyalties completely lacks in empirical evidence.

The government of Mexico is the most visible sector in relations between Chicanos and Mexicans. The government of Mexico has the legitimate right to promote the diffusion and reinforcement of historical knowledge and the values of Mexican culture among its descendents outside of the country. This is a right widely acknowledged by the international community and it is, certainly, a right respected by the government of Mexico when it is exercised by other countries within its national territory. This right ought to be expressly acknowledged by the governments of Mexico and the United States. It should be done in such a manner as to establish rules of the game, free of the suspicion of interference of a political nature in the internal affairs of the one country by the other. There is an enormous potential for concrete benefits to both countries in a clear and constructive relation between United States citizens of Mexican origin and Mexicans.

Chicanos are irreversibly on the way toward becoming participating spokesmen in bilateral relations between Mexico and the United States. Both of us, Chicanos and Mexicans, should aspire to this increased participation that it may become a contribution to a better understanding required by both countries. The geographical proximity and interdependence obligates us not to waste any opportunity to learn to live together based upon mutual respect for national sovereignties and the principles of self-determination for the people.

FOOTNOTES

1. Rodolfo Acuna, *Occupied America:* A History of Chicanos. 2nd ed. Harper and Row, 1981; Luis Arroyo and Victor Nelson-Cisneros. (eds) "Special Issue on Labor History and the Chicano" *Aztlan: International Journal of Chicano Studies Research.* Volume 6 #2 (Summer 1975); Juan Gomez-Quinones, "Mexican Immigration to the United States and the Internationalization of Labor, 1848-1980: An Overview." in Antonio Rios-Bustamante (ed). *Mexican Immigrant Workers in the United States.* Anthology No. 2, Chicano Studies Research Center Publications. MCLA, L.A. 1981, pp. 13-34; Emilio Zamora, "Chicano Socialist Labor Activity in Texas, 1900-1920" *Aztlan* International Journal of Chicano Studies Research. Vol. 6, #2 (Summer 1975).
2. Reies Lopez-Tejerina, *Mi Lucha Por La Tierra* Fondo de Cultura Economico, Mexico D.F., Mexico 1978.
3. Jose Vasconcelos, *La Tesis De La Raza Cosmica.* Mexico, 1928.
4. Octavio Paz, *The Labyrinth of Solitude: Life and Thought in Mexico.* Gross Press. 1982.
5. Carl Allsup, *The American GI Forum.* Center for Mexican American Studies. University of Texas at Austin, 1982.
6. *Zoot Suit*, Peter Burrell, Producer, 1981, Universal Pictures.
7. Carey McWilliams, *Al Norte de Mexico.* Siglo Veintiuno editores, Mexico, D.F. 1968.

THE CHICANO IN MEXICANO-NORTE AMERICANO FOREIGN RELATIONS

Jose Angel Gutierrez

INTRODUCTION

United States foreign policy, as a field of study, does not suffer from a paucity of material describing or analyzing the processes of its formulation. This material, however, tends to focus on the international environment that impacts on United States policy in domestic affairs. Academic concern has been with the decision-making process of institutions within and without the sphere of government; and, moreover, with public opinion and the role of interest groups as both of these contribute to the shaping of policy.[1]

It is the latter category of the literature on foreign policy that is the general focus of this paper, particularly the role of Chicanos in Mexicano-Norte Americano[2] foreign relations. As will be illustrated, ethnic groups have consistently been relegated to the sidelines and are not included in the paradigms of foreign policy formulation as formal interest groups.[3]

This paper is not concerned with measuring the impact that Chicanos have had or ought to have on Mexico-United States relations. It is clear that Chicanos have been involved, are currently engaged in, and will undoubtedly increase their activity in foreign policy matters, particularly in that area dealing with Mexico and Latin America. Rather, this paper will highlight briefly the recent history of relations from 1900 to the present.[4] In tracing the history of the relations between Chicanos and Mexico, the discussion will be limited to contacts between Chicano groups and the President of Mexico.

Chicano groups, as rational, non-state, actors involved in this relationship, have been the focus of other scholars.[5] Here, it is important to examine the traditional models available to U.S. scholars for understanding the foreign policy process. The intent of this examination is to demonstrate the inadequacy of such models for understanding the role of Chicanos in this area.[6] There will then follow a discussion of the main ideological trends within the Chicano community as these, too, have an impact in shaping the relationship. Chicano groups, because of their unique historical experience with both the United States and Mexico, have developed four basic strategies in their relations with the United States and Mexico. These basic strategies stem from philosophical and ideological bases which inform the character of the organizations themselves.

The observations presented in this paper are based upon the author's role as a participant-observer in the relation during the 1970's. Close scrutiny of the material is encouraged.

THE EVOLUTION OF CHICANO CONTACT WITH MEXICO

Contact between Chicanos and the President of Mexico has been an issue in United States-Mexico international relations since the end of official hostilities between the two countries in 1848. With the signing of the Treaty of Guadulupe-Hidalgo, U.S. citizenship was conferred on those persons of Mexican ancestry who chose to remain in the newly ceded territory. Many of them found it difficult to accept the new political and economic order and it was inevitable that they would interject themselves into the continuing dialogue between the U.S. and Mexico. Their grievances included violations of the provisions of the Treaty affecting their land titles, physical violence, labor conflicts with the new Norte American land barons and, in general, a pervasive discriminatory attitude toward Mexicans.[7]

As early as 1850, the Mexican consul in San Francisco protested the application of the Foreign Miner's Tax Law as a violation of the Treaty of Guadalupe-Hidalgo. During this initial period, Mexican consulates were forced to ignore the proscription of interference in the internal affairs of a host country. The consuls felt an obligation toward their former compatriots, and, as such, sought to protect Chicanos from Anglo violence.

However, as domestic affairs in Mexico changed, particularly during the regime of Porfirio Diaz, so too did the policy of protection for the Chicano community change. The changes were brought about by four socio-economic factors. First, the number of Mexicans increased on both sides of the border; second, Chicano attitudes turned against the Diaz regime; third, the political crisis in Mexico spread to all sectors of society; and fourth, the opposition to the Diaz regime organized efforts against the government.[8]

As the opposition toward the Diaz regime became more widespread, the consuls of the administration began taking an adversarial role toward the Chicano-Mexicano population of the United States. Factions and interest groups clashed, often violently, both in Mexico and in the United States, over dominance of the national apparatus of the Mexican state. The *cientificos* in support of Porfirio Diaz saw in the Chicano population a refuge for their political opponents, which included Ricardo and Enrique Magon and Francisco Madero. Mexican police agents hired United States police agents to monitor the activities of opponents to the regime. Not surprisingly, various U.S. government agencies initiated surveillance of Chicano groups on their own.[9]

Following the end of the Mexican revolutionary period in the late 1920s, there came a normalization of relations with Chicanos. In the interim, the persistent pattern of violence and discrimination against Chicanos by Anglos had not diminished. As the stability of the Mexican nation increased, Chicanos and Mexicanos in the U.S. turned once again to the Mexican consuls for protection. By this time, Chicanos had formed their mutual benefit societies and organizations and the consular corps of Mexico represented additional protection and leadership.

The role of the Mexican consulates on behalf of the Chicano and Mexican communities of the U.S., generally, and in Los Angeles, particularly, is detailed by Francisco Balderrama.[10] During the 1930s, Alonzo Perales, founder of the League of United Latin American Citizens (LULAC), frequently sought the assistance of Mexican consuls in efforts for redress of grievances from local authorities in Texas.

Ironically, the contact with the Mexican government by LULAC leaders then and Chicanos now has provided the basis for U.S. government surveillance of the Chicano community. The Federal Bureau of Investigation has monitored the activities of LULAC, among other Chicano organizations, for the past forty years. The contacts with Mexico have been perceived by U.S. government agencies as acts of agents of a foreign government.

The *Bracero* program, begun in 1942 and continuing into the 1960s, dominates the relationship between Mexico and the United States and the Chicano community. As before, the violence, exploitation, and discrimination toward all persons of Mexican ancestry, *braceros* or not, prompted much dialogue and discussion with Mexico. During this period of Chicano-Mexicano relations, the Eisenhower administration implemented its infamous *Operation Wetback* program aimed at the massive deportations and repatriation of Mexicans from the U.S.[11]

During the late 1960s and early 1970s, Chicano activists of the Raza Unida Party began the most recent phase of relations with the President of Mexico. Included in the activity were leaders from older Chicano organizations, such as LULAC, the American G.I. Forum, and the Mexican American Legal Defense and Education Fund (MALDEF). The relations between Chicanos and the Mexican head of state resulted in the Hispanic Commission, *Comision mixta de enlace*,[12] which was formed in the mid-years of the Jose Lopez Portillo administration. The *Comisioń* has not been recognized by the administration of President Miguel de la Madrid. Chicano contact with the present administration has been limited to a summer scholarship program at the Colegio de Mexico.[13]

An interesting aspect of the relations, certainly during the previous two presidential campaigns, has been the role of Chicanos in the election. Both Jose Lopez Portillo and Miguel de la Madrid held various meetings with delegations of Chicano activists, intellectuals, political and community leaders. Beyond the mutual value of publicity and exposure for the candidate, the *Partido Revolucionario Institucional* (PRI), and the Chicano participants, these meetings serve to emphasize the Mexican government's concern for contact and dialogue with Chicano groups.

The meetings during the presidential campaign provide a period of transition for contacts with the outgoing administration and the incoming one. For example, Dr. Jorge A. Bustamante, Bernardo Sepulveda Amor, and Pedro Ojeda Paullada emerge as figures with responsibility to the candidate. Dr. Bustamante serves the current president as the foremost expert on Chicano affairs. Mr. Sepulveda Amor became the Ambassador to the United States and currently is Mexico's Secretary of Foreign Relations. Mr. Ojeda Paullada, who served President Portillo as Secretary of Labor, had the *Comisión* placed under his jurisdiction.

At the meetings during the campaign, issues of concern to Chicanos were presented, in person, to the future president of Mexico. Conversely, the candidate had the opportunity to express his views on the relations between Mexico and Chicanos.

MEXICAN REASONS FOR THE CONTACT

There are concrete reasons for the support extended to the Chicano community by the president of Mexico. Since the 1920s, the social activism of Chicanos mirrors the history of activism in Mexico. Chicanos struggle against the United States government at the local, state, and federal levels, and, they struggle as well against the institutions of white society. Similarly, Mexico struggles against its most significant threat, which is the perceived aggressor to the north, the United States. Intervention in the daily affairs of both Chicanos and Mexicanos stems from United States interests.[14]

The Mexican Revolution of 1910 was aimed, in large measure, at foreign investors and their local partners. This exploitation of Mexican resources began in the 19th century. As the ideological underpinning of the Revolution took hold, the peasantry perceived the local agents of U.S. interests as anti-Mexican and anti-national. The revolutionary spirit with respect to a foreign presence continues to this day. Hence, it is difficult for contemporary Mexicans to ignore or denounce the Chicano struggle for justice. To do so would pose a serious contradiction in nationality and spirit.

There is a continuum of attitude from the *porfiristas* of the 19th century and an element in Mexico today who dismiss the legitimacy of Chicano claims to justice. Briefly, members of the original anti-national class preferred foreign immigrants to the mestizo, promoted Hispanic and European values over the syncretic evolution of indigenous values, invited foreign investment at the expense of local capitalization, favored U.S., British, and German nationals with concessions in natural resources, such as oil, land, and in utilities, communications, and so on. It was these anti-national individuals who played an instrumental part in establishing the client status of Mexico with respect to the United States.

Today, U.S. investments in Mexico exceeds one billion dollars annually. Mexican investment in the U.S., on the other hand, is limited to those who choose to denationalize their currency by maintaining U.S. bank accounts and by purchasing real estate. Former Ambassador, Robert McBride, reports,

> . . . recent activities of business groups in Monterey and Mexico City, there is found a marked eagerness for United States investment . . . the powerful businesses in Monterey have been closely associated with major United States corporations for most of the post-World War II period, as have most of the Mexico City business groups, the working groups of BANAMEX and BANCOMER, and others. The intense desire of the Mexican government to diversify its investment sources in order to prevent 'dependence' on the United States, does not seem to be respected in the attitudes of the private sector.[15]

Anti-Mexicanos are found in Mexico and in the United States militating against closer Chicano-Mexicano relations. Nevertheless, it is safe to say a large number of Mexicans sympathize with the Chicano community for two basic reasons. First, Chicanos tend to maintain family ties to Mexico. The border does not sever family ties, it only separates them. Second, a significant number of Mexicans have worked in the United States. These workers know first-hand the treatment accorded to Chicanos and Mexicanos in the U.S.

The policy of the Mexican government as regards the discriminatory treatment of its citizens and Chicanos has been inconsistent. At times, Mexico has made strong and emphatic protests; and at other times, the response has been weak and ineffectual. Mexico often restrains its genuine concerns for fear of reprisals from the U.S. government. This restraint is perceived by U.S. officials and scholars as cowardice and as disdain for fellow nationals and for their Chicano compatriots.

Mexican presidents, especially since Echeverria, have viewed the Chicano population as a potential source of support for Mexico. As a result, the Mexican president is more accessible to Chicano leaders and organizations than is the President of the United States. In the last ten years, Chicano have had more face-to-face meetings with Mexican presidents, cabinet members, ambassadors, and other high-ranking government officials than they had with their counterparts in the United States.

Since the Echeverria presidency, a wide range of contact and communication between Chicanos and Mexicanos have evolved and the Mexican government has responded positively to issues of concern to the Chicano community. Support has been provided both moral and financial, for immigration policy, medical training, and cultural and educational exchanges.

The broad contact and favorable attitudes on the part of Mexican officials, give Chicanos excellent opportunities to enlist the support of former government officials, academicians, PRI members, elected officials, labor leaders, and even opposition leaders. The experience is invaluable for Chicanos. In effect, the Mexican system provides a training ground on the conduct and processes of national and international affairs.

The potential of Chicano support for Mexico stems from two major sources. The first is in the area of electoral strength. The number of Chicanos in the U.S. Congress nearly doubled from 1970 to 1980. Among the big city majors, Henry Cisneros of San Antonio and Federico Peña of Denver represent electoral strength.

The most dramatic electoral gains, however, continue to occur at the local (city, school, and county) and state levels. Chicano voter registration and actual voting are increasing rapidly, occasionally out-polling white voters. In 1976, only 488,000 Mexican Americans were registered to vote in Texas. By 1980, the figure climbed to 798,563, an increase of 64% in four years. Nationally, the Hispanic voting strength was estimated at 2,646,090 in 1976. In 1980, a comparable estimate places the Hispanic vote at 3,426,990, or a 30% increase.[16] More recently, in the summer of 1983, various major Chicano organizations announced plans for a national voter registration drive with a goal of one million new voters for the 1984 elections.

At the same time, Chicano Democrats, under the banner of "Hispanic Force '84" took advisement the notion of supporting a favorite son, New Mexico's Tony Anaya, in a bid for the presidency. This political strategy was designed to enhance Chicano political leverage within the Democratic Party. A former national president of LULAC, Tony Bonilla, actively campaigned for Jesse Jackson with the hope of forging a viable working relationship between Chicanos and Blacks in electoral contests and Dr. Armando Gutierrez serves as a senior political consultant to Jackson. In the Republican Party, similar but better-financed efforts have begun to increase the Hispanic presence in the Party.

The growing economic power of Chicanos is the second area of support for Mexico. Chicanos and other Hispanic groups spend approximately $70 billion a year on goods and services. In order to reach this growing market, advertisers spent 200 million dollars in 1981.[17] How much Chicanos and Mexicanos temporarily residing in the U.S. spend on goods produced in Mexico for consumption in the

U.S. is difficult to assess. We may assume that the flow of dollars from the U.S. to Mexico through Chicano and Mexicano consumption is extremely important to Mexico.

Finally, among the reasons for Mexican contact with Chicanos is Mexico's progressive foreign policy. Presidents Echeverria and Lopez Portillo have acknowledged the Chicano in the United States as *el Mexico de afuera*, the "other Mexico, outside of Mexico." The implication suggests that Chicanos are an extension of the Mexican people. Both presidents have also included Chicanos as part of the Third World which Mexico purports to represent.[18]

The support of Chicanos on the part of the national leadership of Mexico is another example of Mexico's foreign policy which does not meet with favor among U.S. officials. More examples include Mexico's steadfast refusal to break diplomatic relations with Cuba, the severance of relations with Chile following the overthrow of President Allende, the acceptance of a diplomatic liaison office for the Palestine Liberation Organization (PLO), the financial support of the Sandinista Revolution and the revolutionary government in Nicaragua, and its role in a regional peace initiative, CONTADORA, for a political settlement of conflict in Central America.

ACTORS IN THE RELATIONSHIP

As stated, the traditional models employed in understanding United States foreign policy ignore the role of ethnic minorities. There are six basic paradigms. First, there is the "classic democratic theory" model.[19] It holds that the general public controls the actions of those who make foreign policy. The public, through the ballot, takes rational positions concerning foreign policy issues and then actively support or oppose decision makers. In this model, Chicanos, as would other ethnic groups, do not constitute a significant constituency because of their relatively small percentage in the electorate and their lower than average participation rate at the polls.

Second, the "rational actor" model[20] holds that foreign policy is the result of rational actors taking steps that compliment and support their interests. These actors consider their goals and values, lay out alternative actions, project and evaluate the consequences of each alternative and choose the most beneficial option for their interests, goals, and values. This model is limited to decision makers within U.S. institutions, such as government, the military, and business. Chicanos are inevitably excluded from this model because of their exclusion from the decision making processes within the institutions.

Third, the "organizational-institutional"[21] model stipulates that foreign policy evolves over a period of time. Issues arise and are handled according to the prescriptions of standard operating procedure for the organization or agency within the institution. Complex issues require certain modifications that result in only minor revisions of policy. A broad policy pronouncement is possible as the result of evolutionary, incremental change. Typically, this model is utilized to describe the kind of processes which occur in agencies and organizations within the complex institutions of government, such as the military, the Department of Agriculture, the Department of State, etc. This model is useful for the study of policy changes and the development of policy only when the response is to nonthreatening issues to the security interests of the U.S. This model excludes Chicanos because they constitute a miniscule percentage of government employees and generally are situated at the lower grade levels of Civil Service.

Fourth is the "bureaucratic" model which is utilized to understand the role of appointed public officials in the foreign policy process.[22] This model differs from previous ones in that appointed officials are not elected and neither are they career government employees. Appointed officials are decision makers in complex bureaucracies, civilian and military, who concern themselves with protecting their interests vis-à-vis national economic and security issues. These actors are differentiated from actors in the other models by their motivation. These actors are self-serving in their response to matters at hand. They seek to formulate policy to benefit their narrow interests as opposed to the interest of the general public or that of the national government. This model is useful in analyzing the relationship between appointed officials and their counterparts in the private sector whence they came and where they are likely to return. In this manner, it is possible to assess their role in the end product of the foreign policy process. Needless to say, few Chicanos have been appointed to decision making positions in government agencies. The reasons are clear when one considers that few Chicanos have reached a sufficiently high position in government, business, or labor to receive such an appointment.

The fifth model, "the power elite" was made more popular by President Eisenhower's remark concerning the dangers inherent in the "military-industrial complex" than by C. Wright Mills' treatise on the subject.[23] Mills pointed out that foreign policy is made by an elite group, in and out of government. The power elite constitutes a ruling class and they rule because their interests in business and politics converge and thus alliances are built around the protection and promotion of their interests. Hence, they use their collective power to coerce, in effect, a foreign policy favorable to their collective interests. The power elite does not usually include elected officials, seldom includes appointed officials or bureaucrats, and it is unlikely that one would find a Chicano included in this group.

The sixth and last model is the "pluralist" school found in the discipline of political science.[24] Adherents argue that the entire process of government is akin to an arena in which organized groups with resources compete against one another for the allocation of goods and services. Some groups win and others lose, depending on their skill, resources, and energies. The arena, and more importantly, the process of competition, is assumed to be open, fair, and neutral toward all groups. Because of the plurality of groups able to compete in the process, ethnic minorities are sometimes mentioned in this model as affecting U.S. foreign policy. While ethnic groups are acknowledged as players, the model has a latent potential to endorse only those ethnic groups which mirror bias of the pluralist. If one accepts the notion that the power contest in the political arena is fair, open, and guided by neutral rules, then the process legitimates the particular ethnic as a responsible actor. Failure by ethnic group is perceived to be the result of endemic shortcomings and not the result of defects in the process. Chicano groups have challenged this model because of its bias. Pluralists respond that Chicanos are not "serious" actors in foreign policy because they do not participate when they have nothing to lose and everything to gain from radical activity.

CHICANO REASONS FOR THE CONTACT

Chicano groups are in an interesting position at this historical juncture. Within a reasonable period of time, Chicanos will be able to exercise considerable political control, particularly in the southwestern United States as a result of electoral gains. Chicanos continue to develop, albeit at a different rate, an economic infrastructure to complement their newly-gained political stature.[25] As a result, Chicanos will be able to decide and implement national and international strategies of their own design in the not too distant future.

A dilemma, however, begins to emerge. Chicanos have interposed themselves into the U.S.-Mexico dialogue in order to protect their community interests. The examples of the tuna fish boycott, the Ixtoc well contamination, and the Houston federal case involving educational opportunity for Mexican children, demonstrate the willingness of Chicanos to become involved in issues which have foreign policy implications and this involvement has had a favorable response from Mexico. Chicanos are now subjects of renewed interest in both countries. The dilemma arises from the Chicano presence in the international arena. It appears to raise numerous questions of "loyalty" and "interests" in both countries. For Chicanos, relations with Mexico signify the possibility of the following specific gains:

1. The accessibility of Chicano groups and leaders to the Mexican head of state is a tool of leverage not previously available. Chicanos appear more frequently in the corridors of power in Mexico than they do in the U.S.

2. Consulting and speaking with Mexican officials is an educational process in the exercise of political power and international affairs.

3. The visibility of such high level contact legitimates Chicano leaders, organizations, and strategies, which is useful for social action among constituencies in both countries.

4. Tangible results from these relations, such as scholarships, cultural and educational exchanges, motion picture financing, and library collection donations, are additional resources for the Chicano community.

5. The relations, along with the personal contact serve as an informational conduit to the Chicano community for a Mexican point of view seldom expressed in the U.S.

7. The relations and personal contact has served as an agent of change in the relations among Chicano groups. Meetings with the Mexican presidents has created unity among groups and leaders.[26]

8. Chicanos have begun an examination of their individual and collective motivations with respect to the dialogue with the Mexican government.

This latter point has spurred more reflection among Chicano groups on their political experience as an ethnic minority in the United States. While ideological differences between Chicanos, both organizationally and among individual leaders, have been set aside for the purpose of presenting a united front before the Mexican and United States governments, these differences nevertheless remain and are reflected in the membership of the various organizations, in their statements of mission, goal, and purpose, and in their proposals and positions vis-à-vis issues pertinent to the Chicano and Mexicano communities.

IDEOLOGICAL STRANDS IN THE CHICANO COMMUNITY

There are four major ideological groupings within the Chicano community. These ideologies structure the relationship which various groups develop in their position between Mexico and the United States. First, there are those groups in the Chicano community who perceive themselves to be Mexicanos. These persons construe the border between the two countries as a legal formalism designed to keep apart what is essentially one people and one nation. They seem themselves as an oppressed nationality within the United States, robbed of its cultural and territorial inheritance and kept apart by government and artificial borders. The adherents of this grouping range from internationalists on the left (Marxist-Leninists) to Mexican nationalists.

In the second group are those who recognize the separation of Mexican territory into the United States. These individuals do not perceive themselves to be an extension of the Mexican population; rather, they see themselves as different Mexicanos, i.e., Chicanos—a group apart from both Mexico and the U.S. As a separate and distinct ethnic group, they seek recognition of the ethnic community as almost a separate nationality within the U.S. In real terms, this group seeks support for those programs that would maintain the Chicano ethos. Included in this group are Chicano nationalists and separatists who seek to define the cultural milieu and direction of Chicanos.

Cultural pluralists comprise the third group. This group posits their Mexican ancestry as the basis for the perception of themselves as Third World persons. Along with the recognition of other culturally distinct groups in the U.S., they advocate a multi-cultural society, a mosaic of ethnic groups, with those descended from Third World peoples in the majority. Within this grouping, the concept of the Third World reflects a rejection of capitalism and communism as the economic and political forms of government. They prefer a more balanced form and most of their positions have a humanistic and socialistic tendency. Concretely, they support progressive Democratic Party activity.

The final group consists of individuals and organizations that eschew any connection to Mexico and view their cultural heritage as more symbolic than an active part of their lives. They seek to assimilate as much as possible into what they perceive as the mainstream society. This group would be scattered among traditional Anglo organizations.

Psychologically, this group is the most interesting. Individuals in this group, while they are indeed in the process of assimilation, may be found in organizations within any of the above groupings. This is not as contradictory as it may seem because what causes them to join organizations in the previous categories is not the ideological program but the degree of alienation they experience in their exclusion from mainstream society. In other words, they are clearly identifiable as Mexicans, both physically and culturally, and this prevents their desired assimilation; consequently, they turn to groups which criticize the discrimination imbedded in mainstream society. In a sense, they seek alliances that would facilitate their assimilation.

Chicano organizations choose from this range of philosophy and ideology. Group leaders compete with one another, both within and without each group, for the leadership of the greater community. They employ a variety of ethnic symbols with which to mobilize their own group and other Chicanos. Some leaders, for example, call for Spanish language maintenance, while others call for an open border between the U.S. and Mexico. Such appeals capture the attention of the greater community and serve to mobilize passive individuals. When this happens, the leaders and aspirants to leadership positions will support the symbolic call to action in a manner consistent with their philosophy and ideology.

Certainly, the relationship between Chicano and Mexico does not escape the notice of non-Chicano interests. These non-Chicano interests are better organized, have more resources, and are more powerful.

They seek to diminish the role Chicanos play in the international dialogue with Mexico and they employ a number of methods to restrict Chicano activity. They obtain the cooperation of leaders and members of Chicano organizations, they participate in the repression and annihilation of independent activists and radicals, they coerce and reward certain individuals, and they establish a patron-client relationship in electoral contests. These non-Chicano interests, in the main, prefer the activities of groups that seek assimilation.

The dialogue between Chicano groups and the Mexican president during the last two decades was initiated and continued by leaders of the first two groupings, those who see themselves an extension of Mexico and those who see Chicanos as a distinct cultural entity. The leadership of these two groups, in order to present a greater constituency to the Mexican head of state, formed a tenuous alliance with leaders and members of the other groups, the cultural pluralists and the assimila-tionists. This strategy enhanced the representativeness and appeal of their political program at the same time that the temporary bond provided an opportunity to proselytize their ideology and philosophy to these same groups.

The cultural pluralists and the assimilationists had been quite critical of those who sought and established the dialogue in the early 1970s. In the heat of interne-cine rivalry and at ideological loggerheads, the assimilationists, for example, pub-licly charged the advocates of the dialogue with disloyalty, treason, and a lack of patriotism. However, the greater Chicano community responded favorably to the initiatives, particularly to the gains stemming from the dialogue. The opposition then gave way to a desire to become part of the dialogue.

The coalition of leaders from all four groupings agreed on a common de-mand. This was the establishment, within the Mexican presidency, of a formal mechanism for continuing dialogue; an Office of Chicano Affairs, as it were. It was the assimilationists who lobbied for and were more successful with their agency. Their proposal established the Hispanic Commission and contained a pat-ently exclusionary, self-perpetuating organism of nine Chicano organizations and a Puerto Rican group. Included in the nine Chicano organizations are some without grass roots membership, some dependent on funding from government agencies and foundations, some which are staff-directed and whose locations are outside geographical areas with large Chicano populations.

Three of the organizations are comprised overwhelmingly in their member-ship of professional, career, or federal employees. These are, IMAGE, the Mexican American National Women's Association, and Project SER. Another, the National Association of Farm Worker Organizations, does not include the United Farmworkers of America, the largest farmworker union, founded by Cesar Chavez, or the Arizona Farmworkers Union. The Forum of National Hispanic Organiza-tions is composed of organizations based in Washington, D.C. is staff-directed and heavily dependent upon the support of the Catholic Church. The National Council of La Raza, while making great strides in the direction of membership, grass roots democracy and accountability, nevertheless remains staff-directed and dependent upon the support of the Ford Foundation and other foundation and government grants.

Only two of the nine Chicano organizations, The American G.I. Forum and the League of United Latin American Citizens (LULAC), can be characterized as grass roots, community-based organizations, with rotating leadership and grass roots funding. They have a combined track record of civil rights struggle totalling over a century. LULAC, as a case in point, has made significant strides in the direction of the cultural pluralist category from their assimilationist tendencies of ten years ago. At its 54th Annual National Convention, held in Detroit, Michigan, in July 1983, many resolutions and workshops focussed on international affairs and on United States foreign policy.[27]

CHICANO ACTORS IN THE DIALOGUE

The role of Chicano actors has been noted by other scholars, notably, by Rodolfo O. de la Garza.[28] Scholars have limited the role of Chicano actors in the dialogue to individuals acting in their capacity as academics, businessmen, elected and appointed officials, radicals, and others accepted as representatives of the Chicano community.

Given the recent history of relations between Chicano groups and the Mexican president, professional Chicano academic organizations have not sought to participate in the dialogue. Similarly, the professional organizations of the Chicano business community have not sought participation in the relationship. The two main partisan organizations of elected officials and political party members, the Hispanic American Democrats and the Republican Hispanic Assembly, have not established a relationship with the Mexican government nor with any of the political parties in Mexico. The National Association of Latino Elected and Appointed Officials (NALEO) and the Southwest Voter Registration and Education Project (SVREP) have been invited by members of the Hispanic Commission, but have declined to participate. From 1975 to 1981, while serving as County Judge for Zavala County in Texas, I did participate in the dialogue. More recently, only Mayor Henry Cisneros, of San Antonio, maintains an interest in the dialogue.

The United Farmworkers of America have consistently refused to establish a relationship with the Mexican president, although Cesar Chavez did meet on occasion with President Jose Lopez Portillo and more frequently with Fidel Velasquez, the national leader of the largest Mexican labor union, the Confederacion de Trabajadores Mexicanos (CTM).[29]

The role of intellectuals and elected officials from the Chicano community has been limited to those individuals who accept an invitation to provide consulting services to the campaign of the candidate for president of the PRI.[30]

The role of radicals and other individuals acting as representatives of the Chicano community was eclipsed by the emergence of the Hispanic Commission during the administration of Jose Lopez Portillo. Although some contact with the Mexican president continued the contacts lessened as the Hispanic Commission began to monopolize all organizational contact with the Mexican president. The issues raised during the life of the dialogue between Chicanos and the Mexican presidency continue to be viable concerns for mainstream Chicano politics. Competition for a consolidated leadership of the Chicano community will likely continue unabated, and will likely spring from the four ideological foundations outlined above. Unfortunately, the continuing dialogue with the Mexican presidency is now more narrowly defined by the policies of the Chicano groups who press for their claims.

FOOTNOTES

1. An earlier version of this article was presented as a paper at the XI International Congress of the Latin American Studies Association held in Mexico City, Mexico, September 29-October 1, 1983. On the decision-making process of foreign affairs see, for example, Richard Snyder, H.W. Bruck and Burton Spain, (eds.), *Foreign Policy Decision Making: An Approach to the Study of Foreign Policy Decision-Making*. (New York: Free Press, 1962); Norman R. Luttbeg, (ed.), *Public Opinion and Public Policy*, (Homewood, Ill.: Dorcey Press, 1974); Lars Schoultz, *Human Rights in United States Policy Toward Latin America*, (Princeton: Princeton University Press, 1981).
2. The choice of the Spanish words, *Mexicano* and *Norte Americano* over the English words, Mexican and North American is intentional. One of the many irritants among people on both sides of the border between the United States and Mexico are the labels attached to national origin and ethnic communities. Chicanos, a self-descriptive label, can be both a *Mexicano* by ethnicity and a *Norte Americano* by national origin. Mexicans generally think of Chicanos as *Norte Americanos* referring to their place of birth, their citizenship, much to the chagrin of those Chicanos who take great pride in their cultural Mexicaness. *Norte Americano* to Mexicans means anyone born in the United States of America, regardless of ancestry linking them to Mexico. The Chicano obviously is situated in the context of United States politics and seeks to impact Mexican politics from outside of Mexico.
3. See for example, Lars Schoultz, *Ibid.*
4. A descriptive history of relations between Chicanos and the Mexican President has been my subject in two earlier papers, "Apuntes sobre la historia de relaciones entre Chicanos y el primer mandatario de Mexico: 1972-1978," Mexico-United States Seminar on Undocumented Migration, Centro de Studios Economicos y Sociales del Tercer Mundo, Mexico D.F. Septiembre 4-6, 1980 and "Chicanos and the Mexican President: 1972-1980," Fund for the Improvement of Post Secondary Education—Chicano Studies Research Center, United States—Mexico Conference, Santa Monica, California, April 24-25, 1982. See the forthcoming UCLA Chicano Studies Research Center publication on the subject under the editorship of Emilio Zamora.
5. The most ample discussion of Chicano actors is provided in Rodolfo O. De La Garza, "Demythologizing Chicano-Mexican Relations," in Susan Kaufman Purcell, (ed.), *Mexico-United States Relations, 1981*, Proceedings of the Academy of Political Science, Vol. 34, Number 1, pages 88-96. For a discussion of the *Mexicano* actors see Carlos H. Zazueta, "Mexican Political Actors" in Carlos Vásquez and Manuel Garcia y Griego, (eds.), *Mexican-U.S. Relations Conflict and Convergence* (Los Angeles: UCLA Chicano Studies Research Center Publications and UCLA Latin American Center Publications, 1983), pages 441-482.
6. See Rodolfo O. De La Garza, "Chicano-Mexican Relations: A Framework for Research," *Social Science Quarterly*, March, 1982, Vol. 63, No. 1.
7. See "Part 1 Conquest and Colonization: An Overview" of Rodolfo Acuña, *Occupied America: A History of Chicanos* 2nd ed., (New York Harper & Row Publishers, 1981), and the excellent documentation and analysis of Arnoldo de León *They Called Them Greasers*, (Austin: University of Texas Press, 1983) on the attitudes of Anglos toward Mexicans in Texas.
8. Juan Gomez Quiñonez, "Piedras contra la luna, Mexico en Aztlan y Aztlan en Mexico: Chicano-Mexican Relations and the Mexican Consulates, 1900-1920," in James W. Wilkie et al., *Contemporary Mexico: Papers of the IV International Congress of Mexican History* (Berkeley and Mexico City: University of California Press and El Colegio de Mexico, 1976) pages 495-500.
9. The Committee for Rural Democracy, a Texas based social action agency, developed a

program, the Chicano Legal Defense Fund that made numerous Freedom of Information Act requests on behalf of the Raza Unida Party, the Mexican American Youth Organization, and its leaders. I continued this research effort into the surveillance of other Chicano groups by the United States government. Preliminary research findings and analysis of documents were presented in my paper "Chicanos and Mexicanos Under Surveillance: 1940-1980," at the Texas FOCO conference of the National Association of Chicano Studies at the University of Houston—University Park, February 3-5, 1983.

10. *In Defense of La Raza* (Tuscon: University of Arizona Press, 1982).

11. Attorney General Herbert Brownell, Jr., on June 17, 1954, initiated the program dubbed "Operation Wetback" aimed at preventing the entrance of political subversives, discouraging employers from hiring undocumented Mexicans, encouraging illegal immigrants to leave the United States voluntarily and the deportation of thousands of persons from the United States of Mexican ancestry. During that year, 1954, the Immigration Service [today called Immigration and Naturalization Service (INS)] deported 1,075,000 persons of Mexican ancestry. As per a Freedom of Information Act request of May 27, 1981, the Department of Justice's INS has released to me 1160 pages of official documents relating to this government operation.

12. The Hispanic Commission, as it has been called by the Chicano groups, was placed, structurally, by President Lopez Portillo, under the Secretary of Labor, Pedro Ojeda Paullada. While Chicano groups were glad to have succeeded in lobbying for the establishment of such a commission, the location of this body under Secretary Ojeda Paullada indicated to some groups that Chicano issues were seen only as labor issues related to migratory workers. To others, this location meant proximity to the President among Secretaries making him very attractive as Presidential timber. Membership to the directorate of the Commission was limited to ten (10) organizations from the Chicano and Puerto Rican community. This limitation was a compromise agreement between two groups of Chicano organizations, namely those groups linked with the National Hispanic Forum and those with LULAC. The Hispanic Commission members also agreed to restrict the membership to ten organizations and that changes or additions to the Commission required unanimous approval of its current members. They agreed to rotate quarterly, the Chair for the Commission among the member organizations.

Various meetings took place of the Commission in Mexico City and Washington, D.C. The entire Commission, however, never met with the President. The Secretary of Labor or his representative, Dr. Guido Belsasso, on various occasions reported their dissatisfaction with the activity of the Commission members to the President of Mexico and to other Chicano organizations. The sources of dissatisfaction to the Mexicans was the role of the Catholic church represented by Mr. Pablo Sedillo in the National Hispanic Forum; the exclusion of notable Chicano organizations such as the Raza Unida Party, United Farmworkers of America, the Southwest Voter Registration and Education Project and the National Association of Bilingual Educators; the bitter, internecine struggle between factions within the Commission; the external sources of funding for program activity of some of the member organizations such as Project SER, National Council of La Raza, ASPIRA, and MANA; and the dual role of some organization's leaders, as representatives to the Commission and as members of the United States Department of State Hispanic Advisory Committee. The members of the Commission were: the Puerto Rican group ASPIRA, Project SER, LULAC, American G.I. Forum, MALDEF, National Association of Farmworker Organizations (NAFO), Mexican American Women National Association (MANA), IMAGE, National Hispanic Forum, and the National Council of La Raza. The Commission functioned during the final years of the Lopez Portillo administration and is now defunct.

13. The Mexican Studies summer graduate program at the Colegio de Mexico was initiated by this writer in August, 1978, with President Jose Lopez Portillo. The program operated jointly from the Mexican American Studies Program of the University of Houston—University Park and the Colegio de Mexico. During the 1983 cycle, Chicano

academicians at both institutions coordinated the program, Dr. Armando Gutierrez at Houston and Professor Manuel Garcia y Griego at Mexico City.

14. A most recent and glaring example of United States intervention in the daily affairs of the Mexican people is found in the role of the Federal Bureau of Investigation in Mexico. Under the program name of Border Coverage Project (BOCOV), the FBI carried out activities in Mexico designed to disrupt and destroy organizations and persons determined by the FBI to be suspected Communists, or Communist sympathizers during the years 1961 through 1971. This information was released to this writer under an FOIA request of the Department of Justice.

15. Robert H. McBride, (ed.), *Mexico and the United States* (Englewood Cliffs: Prentice Hall, Inc., 1981), pages 6-7.

16. Chicanos comprise 60% of the Hispanic population category, "Coverage of the Hispanic population of the U.S. in the 1970 Census" Special Studies, p. 23, No. 82, Current Population Report, U.S. Bureau of the Census, Department of Commerce, 1979. This percentage figure does not include the population figures for Puerto Rico. For the source of voter registration data see presentation made by William C. Velasquez and Andrew D. Hernandez entitled, "Paper for Southwestern Political Science Association," March 18, 1982, pages 2-5.

17. Antonio Cuernica "The Hispanic Market: A Profile" *Agenda*, National Council of La Roza, Washington, D.C., Vol. II, No. 3, May/June, 1981, pages 4-7.

18. See my paper presented at LASA, *Ibid.* pages 6-7 and page 13.

19. A brief but cogent analysis of this model can be found in Louis J. Halle's "Foreign Policy and the Democratic Process: The American Experience" in Louis J. Halle and Kenneth W. Thompson *Foreign Policy and the Democratic Process: The Geneva Papers* (Washington, D.C.: University Press of America, 1978).

20. An example of this model is found in Graham T. Allison, *Essence of Decision: Explaining the Missile Crisis*. (Boston: Little Brown, 1971).

21. See John C. Donovan, *The Cold Warriors: A Policy Making Elite* (Lexington, MA.: D.C. Hearth, 1974) for an example of this paradigm.

22. The readings in Don K. Price, *The Secretary of State* (Englewood Cliffs: Prentice Hall, 1960), detail the role of appointed officials in this model.

23. C. Wright Mills, *The Power Elite* (New York: Oxford University Press, 1956), the work of G. William Dormhoff *Who Rules America* (New York: Prentice Hall, 1967) and that of Thomas R. Dye *Who's Running America?* 2nd Edition, (New York: Prentice Hall, 1983) are good examples of this model.

24. See Samuel Huntington's discussion of the pluralist paradigm in his *American Politics: The Politics of Disharmony* (Cambridge, MA: The Belknap Press, 1981) pages 5-10.

25. The entire issue of *Nuestro* January/February, 1979, is dedicated to Latino business and finance. On pages 23-28, a listing of the top 100 businesses, banks and savings and loans and their wealth is provided.

26. Both President Echeverria and Lopez Portillo often insisted on meeting with a delegation that would include all interests of the Chicano community and their leader, instead of one person representing all. They assumed early on in their meetings with different Chicano groups that the plurality of organization, leaders and interests actually reflected a disunity of purpose and mind. To date this diversity perplexes the Mexican officials as much as it frustrates friends and foes of Chicanos in the United States who insist on a simple statement about Chicano issues, their problems and wants from one source, that *one* Chicano leader of all Chicanos. Increasingly, decision makers in both countries are becoming more aware of the diversity within the Chicano community simply being a microcosm of the greater diversity within the greater society.

27. For examples of these resolution, workshops and agenda see *LULAC Issues Brief Book* prepared by the LULAC national staff for the convention issued June 29, 1983. LULAC also publishes a monthly magazine for its membership and interested subscribers, *LATINO*, that reflects the cultural pluralist tendency with remnants of assimilationist ideology.

28. op. cit.

29. Cesar Chavez declined invitations by this writer, Reis Lopez Tijerina, Eduardo Morga and others to participate in the dialogue with President Luis Echeverria. Since that time, Chavez has begun with the cooperation of Mexican labor unions, some affiliated with the CTM, to attempt the organizing of Mexican workers in Mexico prior to arrival in California.

30. A major concern of the De La Madrid campaign was to avoid the charge that meeting with Chicanos during the campaign was purely symbolic and self-serving. To avoid this charge, the staff proposed to hold three meetings between Chicanos and the candidate, two during the campaign and one after the election. The first two meetings were for intellectuals and scholars and for elected and appointed public officials. The final meeting was to be with leaders of major Chicano organizations and independent national figures not affiliated with a national organization. This latter meeting never took place, according to Ricardo Valero acting for the campaign as the Director of International Relations, because of the severe economic hardships facing Mexico, the government, and the PRI. Curiously enough, Chicanos often have traveled at their own expense to meetings in Mexico.

CHICANOS AS AN ETHNIC LOBBY: LIMITS AND POSSIBILITIES

Rodolfo O. De La Garza

The role Chicanos should play in U.S.-Mexican relations inevitably raises certain political issues. Central to these issues is Chicano-Mexican relations. This paper then, will have two objectives. In the first, it will provide additional information in support of themes and propositions presented in previously published studies [de la Garza 1980; 1981b; 1982a]. Second, it will attempt to clarify ambiguities persisting in those studies. There are six previously raised issues which require further discussion.

1. What is Mexico's obligation to Chicanos?
2. What are the constraints within which Chicano-Mexican relations are developing?
3. Who are the actors involved?
4. What are the issues around which the relationship might evolve?
5. What is the saliency of ethnic vs. state interests?
6. What are the likely consequences of this relationship for Chicanos and for Mexicans and the Mexican state during the foreseeable future?

These questions are related and there is a tendency for them to overlap. However, it is important to isolate them sufficiently to address each separately. The first question above is not easily discernible in the previous studies and therefore will be dealt with first.

It should be noted that the focus of this paper falls on the particularity of relations between all types of Chicano actors and Mexican governmental actors (de la Garza, 1982a: 117-121). Interaction between non-governmental actors and Chicano groups is varied and is increasing. It is reasonable to argue, though, that overall significance of these relations is considerably less important than interaction where government actors are involved (de la Garza, 1981b: Zazueta, 1980: 22). If these unofficial contacts increase in significance, it is doubtful that they will be allowed to continue without official intervention. It is safe to assume that either Mexican or U.S. authorities will bring them within their purview.

I. *Mexico's Obligations to Chicanos*

Normative theorists have long wrestled with the meaning of political obligation. Given the existence of the nation-state system, it would seem useful in this analysis to focus on the meaning of obligation from within that context. Furthermore, because the discussion here concerns Chicano-Mexican relations, the primary questions are: first, does a state have an obligation to non-citizens who share historic cultural ties and does a state have obligations to citizens beyond its borders; and second, do non-citizens of a state living beyond its borders have an obligation to that state and do non-citizens have an obligation to citizens of that state, independent of their obligation to the state, because of a shared culture? The answer to both sets of questions is no and yes, respectively.

The obligation of a state to its citizens beyond its border are clear. So long as an individual has not surrendered his citizenship, he is guaranteed all rights of citizenship when he returns to his state. Furthermore, while abroad the individual may look to representatives of his state's consular corps to insure he enjoys all the rights and protections due him under the laws of the host state.

The obligations of a state to non-citizens outside its border are not so clear. Indeed, to suggest that such an obligation exists, however intimate the cultural or racial ties may be, seems in itself a radical proposition given the nature of the nation-state system. States, by definition, have limited resources, limited authority and a limited sphere of influence. To suggest that states have obligations to non-citizens across the globe conjures up images of continual intervention and chaos. Indeed, it was a variant of this proposition that was used to legitimize "Dollar Diplomacy," Hitler's expansionist policies, and imperialism. Given that there is little or no theoretical literature to support such a position, it must be concluded that states do not have such an obligation and, therefore, it follows that Mexico has no political obligation to Chicanos.

Immediately after 1848, Mexico in fact *did* have an obligation to insure that the rights and privileges of its former citizens would be protected. This was an obligation imposed on Mexico by treaty and one honored with a vigor that belied its weakened position (de la Garza, 1980: 575). Since then, however, Mexico has had no obligation to Chicanos. U.S. government agencies have had a history of offering no protection to Chicanos. Chicanos, then, have turned to Mexican consuls as if Mexico in fact had a policy of protecting Chicano rights. The context in which these contacts were made indicate that Chicanos turned to Mexican authorities as a last resort more so than because of the perception that Mexican officials had a duty to assist them. Moreover, conditions at the time were such that distinguishing between Mexican citizens and U.S. citizens of Mexican origin was conceptually and emprically impossible. Thus, Mexico's obligation to protect the rights of its citizens in this country carried over to the benefit of Chicanos (Zazueta, 1980: 11-12; de la Garza, 1980: 576).

Today, the distinction between Mexicans and Chicanos is conceptually very clear to Mexican officials and to the Mexican public. "The Mexicans, the average Mexican not to mention official government representatives, make that clear distinction between what is a Chicano and what is a Mexican national in the United States" (del Castillo, 1982: 6). This enables Mexico to protect the maltreatment of undocumented workers while abstaining from becoming embroiled in internal Chicano civil rights disputes.

36

At least one Mexican academic insists that Mexico does indeed have an obligation to Chicanos. Carlos Zazueta argues that Mexico has an "historical responsibility" to Chicanos and that it cannot ignore these people. Mexico must accept its "official responsibility." The basis of this obligation appears to Zazueta to derive from continued emigration of Mexicans to the United States [Zazueta, 1980].

Zazueta does not indicate what this "official responsibility" means in terms of action the Mexican government must initiate on behalf of Chicanos vis-à-vis state and national institutions in the United States. Indeed, his formulation seems limited to rights and privileges Chicanos will accrue in Mexico. According to the conclusion in Zazueta's analysis, Chicanos and Mexicans would have equal rights in Mexico but not in the United States. This would be clearly disadvantageous to Mexicans and the Mexican government is not likely to accept it.

Zazueta goes so far as to advocate that Chicanos be given special privileges up to and including dual citizenship. They "cannot be considered foreigners." At the same time, however, he acknowledges that Chicanos have assimilated much of the Anglo-Saxon world view and are thus culturally distinct, at least in part, from Mexicans [Zazueta, 1980].

This view is apparently shared by several Chicano academics and activists as well. A professor at the *Instituto del Tercer Mundo* actively involved in Chicano-related research spoke with surprise at his experience with Chicanos who went to Mexico expecting to enlist not only interest in, but support for Chicano causes. He observed that this was the first time in his experience that an ethnic group from the U.S. had gone to the motherland seeking help rather than offering it.

Only those who argue an obligation on the part of Mexico toward Chicanos can expect Mexico to act on behalf of Chicano interests, and could criticize Mexican officials for not acting in support of Chicano causes. On the other hand, those who accept that Mexico has no obligation to Chicanos, are in no position to criticize Mexico for its lack of political support of Chicano issues.

Citizens of one state similarly have no obligation to a state where they are not citizens. To suggest otherwise is to undermine the foundations of citizenship through naturalization, not to mention birthright, and to make meaningless the rights of individuals to emigrate and to live wherever they choose. It could, for example, lead to such ridiculous situations as having El Salvadorean refugees obligated to pay taxes to the government they fled. Legal resident-aliens are in similar though not identical situations. At minimum, they have the obligation to maintain political allegiance to their current state of residence and to abide by laws and institutions so long as these fall within the limits of internationally accepted standards of governance.

The obligations of culturally linked non-citizens to citizens of another state, as in the case of Chicanos and Mexicans, is a more complex issue. As a culturally linked ethnic group, it may be argued that Chicanos have a fiduciary obligation to the maintenance of Mexican culture (Parsons, 1975: 61-62). Given the dynamic nature of ethnicity, this may not be taken to mean that Chicanos must preserve Mexican culture as it was at some fixed moment in time, even if that were possible. Whatever the ethnic obligation may be, it culturally binds Chicanos to the Mexican people and not to the Mexican state. If this is so, then Chicanos may have an obligation to act on behalf of Mexican culture and hence the Mexican people when policies by any agency or individuals threaten the integrity of the culture or the people. This means clearly that Chicanos under certain circumstances would have an obligation to protest the actions of either the Mexican or U.S. government when either initiates efforts that threaten the culture of the people. In the U.S., this means Chicanos *should* protest efforts to eradicate the Spanish language; in Mexico, this means they *should* protest the disruption of Indian communities in Mexico's Southeast.

The basis for developing relations with the Mexican state must be kept distinct from the basis upon which relations with the Mexican people are developed. However binding and intimate relationships become between Chicanos and Mexicans as a people, Chicanos, it must be stressed, have no obligation to the Mexican state. The obligation, if any exists, is to the Mexican people and to Mexican culture.

II. *The Constraints of the Relationship*

It has been argued previously that Mexico faces two principal constraints in its relations with Chicanos. First, there is the tradition of non-interference in the internal affairs of foreign states. Second, there is the economic dependence on U.S. trade, loans, and investment [de la Garza, 1980: 574]. It was further argued that Mexico's new found oil wealth could generate increased policy space which could lead to an increasingly active and independent foreign policy in general, and to increasing freedom in determining relations with Chicanos [de la Garza, 1982a: 117].

Zazueta also arrived at strikingly similar conclusions. However, he is more explicit in warning of the risks Mexico faces in pursuing Chicano ties too diligently. "Mexico's historic responsibility to the Chicano people has limits, and, to a great degree, those limits are imposed by the United States and, more correctly, the nature of the relationship between the two countries. (Given the inequalities in the relationship) the least that could be expected would be reprisals from Washington" [Zazueta, 1980:46].

For these and other reasons, the increased options available to Mexico as a function of its new role as an oil giant do not seem sufficient to predict that relations with Chicanos will venture beyond the cultural and symbolic realms [de la Garza, 1980: 581; 1982a: 126]. Two events, which may or may not be related, bear this out. In the first, the premise that Mexico would become increasingly independent because of its oil bonanza is, for the foreseeable future, no longer viable. Where once Mexico was in a position to choose among buyers, now it is in the unfortunate position of seeking a stable and guaranteed market. The United States is the most likely to fill that role. Overall, Mexico is today more dependent on the United States than it has been in decades, and that means that its policy space has been proportionately diminished (Dominguez, 1982: 190-91; Purcell, 1982: 384-85).

Second, and more important, President de la Madrid has publicly described the direction and limits of Chicano-Mexican relations. According to Jorge Bustamente, President de la Madrid stated that "the central objective of these relations is the extension and strengthening of knowledge and understanding of Mexican culture among Mexican descendents that live in the United States . . . He limited the relations of his government to cultural areas, excluding the political" [Bustamante, 1982]. This is a position far different from that allegedly taken by President Lopez Portillo (Gutierrez, 1980: 23). An analysis of Mexican government activities involving Chicanos shows that even under the presidency of Luis Echeverria they were largely restricted to educational and cultural areas. Echeverria, like his successors afterward, eschewed political entanglements in his relations with Chicanos. His views may be characterized as follows, "I can do some things for Chicanos, but you have to realize that you are Americans and you have to solve your own problems" [del Castillo, 1982: 5].

President de la Madrid has defined the boundaries of Chicano-Mexican relations in the terms previously suggested; that is, in terms of symbolic obligations. Jorge Bustamente concludes that the idea of the Mexican government looking to Chicanos as a lobby has been "discarded from the panorama of objectives of the relations between the government of Mexico and Chicanos" (Bustamante, 1982). As Bustamante goes on to note, this is in stark contrast to the claims made by various Chicanos that Chicanos would serve in this capacity or that Mexico viewed Chicanos in such a way (Gutierrez, 1980: 32).

The constraints under which Chicanos live remain constant. They still have not achieved the political influence sufficient to make them a powerful voting bloc except under certain conditions (Garcia and de la Garza, 1977: 100-120). They continue to vote at lower rates than Anglos (Brischetto, Aviña and Doerfler, 1982) and although they have added three more Congressmen to the Chicano delegation in the 1982 elections, they still do not command great influence in Washington (de la Garza, 1982b). Anglo officials continue to react to the suggestion of improved Chicano-Mexican relations as an implicit threat to U.S. interests. In response to a general question regarding the role Chicanos might play in U.S.-Mexican relations, Ambassador John Gavin admonished Chicanos to understand that they are Americans and that it would be impolitic to engage in any activities with Mexico that do not reflect this realization or perspective. The sharpness of his reaction suggests the suspicion with which public officials view even the most innocent of Chicano initiatives in Mexico [de la Garza, 1980: 579].

Although President de la Madrid's statement seems to obviate the need for further discussion, it is useful to keep addressing the issues in view of changing conditions.

III. *The Actors*

Recent events and analyses by a number of researchers support the view of relatively few actors involved in the development of Chicano-Mexican relations. While Lopez Portillo and de la Madrid have met with a variety of Chicanos, these meetings have more and more been limited to members of elite political, academic and economic circles (Zazueta, 1980; Bustamante, 1982). As was stated in 1979, the Chicanos attending these meetings are not "able to claim that they are acting in response to any kind of popular mandate" (de la Garza, 1980: 580). At least one academic, for example, who was initially approached about participating in these meetings was quickly excluded from further consideration. He alleges that the exclusion came as a consequence of his questioning why Chicanos should be interested in developing relations with representatives of the *Partido Revolucionario Institucional*, given its history on civil rights, economic redistribution, political corruption, and repression. Although a variety of Mexican actors could become involved in these relations, it seems that the principal actors will be associated with the government.

39

Zazueta (perhaps the only Mexican scholar to have researched and published on Chicano-Mexican relations) agrees with these assessments. He states that relations will necessarily be restricted to a "few individuals, above all those belonging to the elite on both sides" (Zazueta, 1980: 40). He expresses some confidence in knowing who these actors will be in Mexico, but he is uncertain about the Chicanos. "On the one hand we know that the Mexican government is the principal on that (the Mexican) side of the border. This does not mean, necessarily, that it is the only Mexican actor, just the most important one. On the other side it is more difficult to establish who will be the principal actor for the Chicano community" (Zazueta, 1980:2).

To date, then, there is no evidence to suggest that non-governmental actors in Mexico are taking a significant role in Chicano-Mexican relations. Nor is there evidence to support the notion that the Chicano community as such has become mobilized around any issues related to Mexican national or international life. As with other Americans, Chicanos may be aware of the serious economic problems facing Mexico, and, unlike other Americans, they may be much more sympathetic to Mexico. However, this does not suggest that such issues are of sufficient importance to mobilize the Chicano community on Mexico's behalf. Neither does it suggest a successful response from the community to the efforts of some Chicano leaders to mobilize in that direction [de la Garza, 1982a: 123-126].

IV. *Linkage Issues*

It has been argued (de la Garza, 1980; 1982a; Gutierrez, 1980; Bustamante, 1982) that the principal types of issues around which Chicano-Mexican linkage will develop are cultural and largely symbolic. Mexico continues to support the *Becas de Aztlan Program* and other cultural exchanges. Chicanos are clearly willing to participate in and to expand these types of initiatives. As indicated above, President de la Madrid, as a matter of policy, has limited official Mexican activities to these areas.

Advocates of expanded Chicano-Mexican relations have suggested a major substantive issue, immigration, around which these bonds might be strengthened. The Chicano community has not been of one voice on this issue (de la Garza, 1980). Though Chicanos as a whole are less critical of undocumented workers than Anglos seem to be, there is still a significant proportion of Chicanos who are critical of or opposed to the presence of undocumented workers in the United States (de la Garza, 1981a; Peterson, 1982). Recent studies indicate that Mexican workers and Chicanos show few signs of ethnic solidarity, and both groups are very conscious of the distinctions between them. Chicanos and Mexicans prefer to work and socialize primarily with members of their own group (Nunez and Rodriguez, 1982). For these reasons, assumptions that point to the undocumented worker issue as an automatic basis for linking Chicanos and Mexican are tenuous at best.

It has also been suggested that the cultural programs sponsored by the Mexican government will serve as a basis for linking Chicanos to Mexico. While such contacts are clearly in the interests of both groups, they have the potential for protests and criticism which may prove embarrassing for the Mexican government (Gutierrez, 1980: 13). Rodolfo "Corky" Gonzales, for example, was extremely critical of efforts by Jose Angel Gutierrez to develop relations with the Mexican government. He construed such actions as "support for a fascist Mexican government and a betrayal of the Mexican people" (Acuna, 1981: 389). At the scholarly level, the ongoing studies by Alejandro Saragoza (1981) and Jose Limon (1983) are also sharply critical of Mexican political practices. Both address the question of major Mexican intellectuals and the film industry, perhaps unintentionally, helping to legitimize the policies developed by the Mexican government since 1940, policies which have led to the most inequitable income distribution pattern in Latin America. It should not surprise anyone if Mexican officials were to chafe under such criticism, particularly when they come from Chicanos (del Castillo, 1982: 4).

These are the salient issues for key actors on both sides of the border (de la Garza, 1982a). While specific linkages may develop around specific problems or concerns in the future, at the moment there is no evidence for anything but the issues mentioned.

V. *Ethnic vs. State Interests*

Given that Mexico has no political obligation to Chicanos, it would follow that Mexico will pursue relations with Chicanos so long as it is in its interest to do so. The cultural bonds that exist between the Mexican state and Chicanos are not sufficient to overcome state interests. Stated differently, Mexican officials will respond to Chicano interests only when they stand to benefit from such activity. Conversely, they will oppose Chicano interests whenever these conflict with state interests. In effect, Mexico will pursue relations with Chicanos in the same way it pursues relations with other groups. Since the Mexican state does not have obligations to Chicanos different from its obligations to other groups beyond its borders, it is reasonable, predictable, and appropriate that the Mexican state act only in its own best interest. Several examples will illustrate this pattern.

Historically, Mexican governments have dealt with Chicanos in obviously self-serving ways. Anglo (Harris and Sadler, 1978), Mexican (Zazueta, 1980), and Chicano (Gomez Quinones, 1976; de la Garza, 1980), scholars are in agreement on this point. Zazueta describes policy in the 19th and early 20th centuries by saying that "it isn't even possible to speak of an ambivalent policy, but rather there was an opportunistic policy designed and one more element of internal Mexican political struggles" [Zazueta, 1980: 16].

Mexico's unwillingness to accept a Chicano ambassador until 1979 is part of the same pattern. Mexico, as do all other states that see themselves as being influential in regional or world affairs, expects that American representatives assigned to Mexico will have a status sufficient to facilitate communications with the White House and the State Department. Since Chicanos are not powerful domestic actors as a group, and since no Chicano has had intimate personal ties to any president such as Andrew Young to Jimmy Carter, Mexico considered it a slight to have a Chicano appointed as ambassador. Until the appointment of Julian Nava, Mexico's position could be stated as follows: "Send us ambassadors who are influential. Do not send us ambassadors chosen to resolve your domestic political situation." Mexican analysts correctly interpreted the appointment of Nava stemming from precisely these reasons (Centro de Investigacion y Docencia Economica, 1980).

Although Mexico accepted the Nava appointment, Mexican officials will continue to prefer non-Chicano appointees until such time as Chicanos have either the political or personal clout to be influential among top-level American decision makers. A Mexican scholar describes the Mexican perspective, ". . . (officially)

Mexicans want a true American and they know well the sort of subordinate role that many Chicanos have played in the political and social affairs of the United States . . . Mexicans must be dealing with people that have the proper connections . . . Mexicans unfortunately want an Anglo ambassador" (del Castillo, 1982: 3).

American officials, particularly career foreign service officers, have long understood and have been sympathetic to Mexico's position. Foreign service officers resent the use of ambassadorships for domestic political payoffs. They consider political appointees unqualified. Also, host nations often voice private displeasure to them. This has been particularly true with "ethnic" appointments, that is, the practice of naming Black or Spanish-surnamed ambassadors to nations in Africa or Latin America. According to State Department officials, one African state complained that it would accept no more U.S. Black ambassadors until the United States appointed a Black ambassador to France.

Similarly, State Department officials claim that during the Carter administration, a South American government refused to act on the appointment of a Puerto Rican nominee. Officials for the government in question did not formally declare the appointee unacceptable. They simply never accepted his credentials. After considerably delay, the nominee's credentials were recalled, but the government was then informed that it would accept the next candidate or no ambassador would be named. This incident was exacerbated by the fact that the nominee was a personal friend of the Secretary of State.

Chicano and Anglo leaders have long known of Mexico's views in this regard. Congressman Henry B. Gonzalez has publicly criticized this policy. Stories are rife concerning the efforts of Mexico to prevent the appointment of Chicano ambassadors. The principal Chicano candidate for such an appointment early in the Carter administration reports that his appointment was dropped because of official Mexican opposition. This opposition is never publicized, instead, it threads its way through informal communications channels.

A member of the *Secretaria de Relaciones Exteriores* attests to the existence of such opposition. However, with the exception of this individual and Jorge Bustamente, Mexican academics refuse to either comment on or acknowledge this opposition by Mexico to Chicano diplomats. A senior level member of the *Secretaria* under Lopez Portillo is reported to have been insulted by Julian Nava's appointment. He allegedly remarked, "Just because he looks like us, they think he will be more acceptable to us." The comment is ironic because it was made by an official charged with U.S. affairs. As the official is of European rather than mestizo origin, his remarks are said to have elicited the following response, "Isn't that why they appointed you to deal with U.S. affairs?"

Mexico, it must be stressed, has an obligation to its internal and foreign policy interests and not to Chicanos. Thus, Mexico has every right to demand the United States send ambassadors who have the political and professional credentials sufficient to handle ever-increasing complex relations with the United States. To date, Chicanos have not had this type of political power. Further, very few Chicanos have advanced professionally to a level sufficient to meet these requirements. Thus, Mexico has justifiably opposed Chicano appointments. As Chicano political power increases and as more individuals acquire the appropriate credentials, there is no doubt that Chicano ambassadors will be acceptable to Mexico; in fact, they may be desired. Until both conditions are met, Mexicans will "unfortunately want an Anglo ambassador" (del Castillo, 1982: 3).

A third example of Mexican self-interest which over-rides and counters Chicano interests may be found in the case of the *Asociacion de Reclamantes* vs. the Mexican government. The background and evolution of this case has been described elsewhere (Salazar, 1981). The focus here will be only on recent issues which illustrate the argument.

As recently as 1980, representatives of the *Asociacion*, including myself, met with one of President Lopez Portillo's advisors to suggest a way to resolve this long standing dispute. At the meeting, he was presented with a plan which would have met all the needs of the claimants, cost the Mexican government almost nothing economically given present and foreseeable economic conditions, and transferred all substantial costs to the American public in a relatively painless way.

Prior to the meeting, the proposal was discussed with several individuals, including a member of the *Secretaria de Relaciones Exteriores* and another individual who sometimes was consulted by Lopez Portillo for advice on specific matters. Their reaction produced comments such as, "creative, ingenious, it might work, it's risky." The President's advisor reacted initially by asking if the meeting had been cleared with the U.S. ambassador. The group was confident that American officials would object to the idea, although it was perfectly legal. The advisor was told that the group did not think it necessary to clear its business through the embassy; he responded with a "maybe so, maybe not" gesture. He went on to observe that the plan carried political risks. Mexico, he said, has many friends in the U.S.—Chicanos being only one group of them. He would not want to recommend action that could arouse the ire of these other friends. He concluded the meeting by saying he found the plan intriguing and would think about how he should handle it. The Asociacion did not hear from the Lopez Portillo administration. Suit was filed in Federal District court in Washington where a decision is now pending.

The arguments presented in the opening hearing of the trial are instructive. First, Mexico does not deny the validity of the claims. The judge stated, "There's no question in my mind that they've (the plaintiffs) not been treated as they should be." ". . . It's a recognized debt, as far as I can see, of the Mexican government." Mexico's attorney acknowledges the debt: "I think we have an acknowledged debt by the Mexican government to these claimants . . ." "Can it really be doubted that the Mexican nation owes some money—I don't know how much . . ." However, Mexico argues that it is a diplomatic issue which ought to be settled through diplomatic channels. Mishandling it could "foul up the foreign relations of the United States . . ." The judge, however, responded to this argument by asking: "How do you say that they can keep going back to the diplomats or back to Mexico, hat in hand. Aren't they really being denied their rights that they have established under this treaty?" [Asociacion de Reclamantes, 1983].

Mexico's attempt to use diplomatic channels to resolve the issue is most instructive. By using diplomatic channels there is a better possibility to exert influence in dismissing the suit; whereas, in the courts they have already conceded several legal points which reduces their argument, and hence their influence, to nil. According to senior State Department advisors, Mexican officials have on at least two occasions asked the State Department to intervene on its behalf to dismiss the suit. In other words, the issue is between Mexico and Chicanos. By attempting to move the issue into diplomatic channels, they are asking U.S. officials to assist them in the dismissal of a multi-million dollar debt they have already acknowledged that Mexico owes to the Chicano claimants.

Again, the point here is not to condemn Mexico's actions. Rather, it is to show that Mexico, when in conflict with Chicanos, will pursue its own interests, as any state will. At bottom, Mexico will pursue its interest whether they be to the benefit or to the detriment of Chicanos.

VI. *Consequences of Chicano-Mexican Relations*

As demonstrated above, for the foreseeable future Chicanos will not play a major role in U.S.-Mexican relations and Chicano-Mexican relations will not be an important factor in bilateral negotiations. As has been argued, there are some circumstances around which Chicano-Mexican bonds may expand and become more important, but these will be exceptions to a general rule.

It is also important to emphasize that most of the activities that will continue between Chicanos and Mexican will occur outside the purview of state concerns. While these may help create bonds between groups, they may also serve to divide groups. Furthermore, if such contacts evolve into important areas, U.S. and Mexican officials are sure to become involved.

Thus, Chicanos do not appear to be in a position to become important independent actors in this arena. Their principal contribution may be the vantage point from which to assist each side to understand the other [de la Garza, 1982a: 129]. Carlos Zazueta similarly concludes that Chicanos "may become the natural 'broker' between two worlds that are so different." Further, he does not anticipate that Chicanos will play an important role in bilateral relations. "Thus, the importance of Chicanos in the context of relations between Mexico and the United States for the present decade will not be of great impact . . . Whatever closeness develops between Mexico and Chicanos will have a secondary lateral effect on Mexico-U.S. relations" [Zazueta, 1980].

Chicanos and Mexicans should continue and expand their relations so that both may come to understand fully what they share and how they differ. Chicanos should approach the Mexican government with even greater caution than they approach the U.S. government. The latter, after all, has real and permanent obligations to Chicanos while Mexico has none. Furthermore, in minimal practical ways and clear philosophical grounds, Chicanos may hold U.S. officials accountable. There are no grounds on which to hold Mexican officials accountable. In other words, as a worst case analysis, Chicanos may be poorly served by the U.S. government but they have a right to expect and demand their rights are recognized and protected. Chicanos have no grounds on which to expect or demand anything from the Mexican government.

Ethnic and cultural affinities place Chicanos in an excellent position to understand both Mexico and the United States. Clearly, they have a role to play in U.S.-Mexican relations. Chicanos, more than any other group, may help to explain and interpret how each sees the other and to suggest ways to reconcile differences. In the event they do play this role, however, Chicanos must become knowledgeable about the intricacies of bilateral relations and U.S.-Mexican interests. They must be prepared to discuss pertinent issues realistically, recognizing that the policies of both governments are subject to criticism when circumstances so warrant.

BIBLIOGRAPHY

Asociación de reclamantes, et al., Plaintiffs vs. The United Mexican States, Defendant. Civil Action #81-2299. January 13, 1983 [Transcript].

Acuña, Rodolfo. *Occupied America: A History of Chicanos*. New York: Harper & Row, 1981, Second Edition.

Brischetto, Robert R., Annette Aviña, and Yolanda Doerfler. *Mexican American Voting in the 1982 Texas General Election*. San Antonio, Texas: Southwest Voter Registration Education Project, December, 1982.

Bustamante, Jorge. "Relacion cultural con los Chicanos," *Uno Mas Uno*, October 11, 1982, p. 2.

De la Garza, Rodolfo O. "Chicanos and U.S. Foreign Policy: The Future of Chicano-Mexican Relations," Western Political Quarterly, XXXIII, No. 4 (Dec. 1980), pp. 571-582.

De la Garza, Rodolfo O. "Chicano Political Elite Perceptions of the Undocumented Worker: An Empirical Analysis," Working Papers in U.S.-Mexican Studies, 31 (San Diego: University of California Program in U.S.-Mexican Studies). 1981a.

De la Garza, Rodolfo O. "Demythologizing Chicano-Mexican Relations," in Susan Kaufman Purcell, ed. *Mexico-U.S. Relations* (New York: American Academy of Political Science): pp. 88-96. 1981b.

De la Garza, Rodolfo O. "Chicano-Mexican Relations: A Framework for Research," *Social Science Quarterly*, Vol. 63, No. 1 (March, 1982a), pp. 115-130.

De la Garza, Rodolfo O. "And Then There Were Some . . . Chicanos as National Political Actors, 1967-1980," Mexican American Studies, The University of Texas at Austin, Texas. 1982b.

Del Castillo, Gustavo. Interview. "Chicanos in the U.S.-Mexican Relationship," Fronteras Program #117: California State University at San Diego. June 27, 1982.

Dominguez, Jorge I. "International Reverberations of a Dynamic Political Economy," Jorge P. Dominguez, ed. Mexico's Political Economy: Challenges at Home and Abroad, Beverly Hills, California: Sage Publications, 1982, pp. 171-233.

García, F. Chris, and Rodolfo O. de la Garza. *The Chicano Political Experience*. Duxbury, Massachusetts, 1977.

Gomez-Quiñones, Juan. "Piedras contra la luna. Mexico en Aztlan y Aztlan en Mexico: Chicano-Mexican Relations and the Mexican Consulates, 1900-1920." in James W. Wilkie, Michael C. Meyer and Edna Morgan de Wilkie, (eds.), *Contemporary Mexico: Papers at the IV International Congress of Mexican History.* (Berkeley: University of California Press, 1976), pp. 494-528.

Gutierrez, José Angel. "Apuntes sobre la historia de relaciones entre grupos chicanos y el primer mandatorio de Mexico: 1972-1980." Paper presented at the Mexico-U.S. Seminar on Undocumented Migration. Mexico City, 1980.

Harris, Charles N., III and Louis R. Sadler. "The Plan of San Diego and the Mexican-United States War Crisis of 1916: A Reexamination," *Hispanic American Historical Review*, 58(August, 1978): pp. 381-408.

Límon, José. "Mexicans and Speech Play: Ideology and Interpretation." University of Texas, Austin, Texas. 1983.

Nuñez, Rogelio and Nestor Rodriguez. "Theoretical Explorations of Chicano-Indocumentado Relations." Paper presented at the Conference on Mexican Immigration and the Mexican American Community, University of Texas at Austin, October, 1982.

Parson, Talcott. "Some Theoretical Considerations on The Nature and Trends of Change of Ethnicity" in Nathan Glazer and Daniel P. Moynihan (eds.) *Ethnicity: Theory and Experience*, Harvard University Press, Cambridge, 1975.

Peterson, Robert A. and George Kozmetsky. "Public Opinion Regarding Illegal Aliens in Texas," *Texas Business Review* (May-June, 1982), pp. 118-121.

Purcell, Susan Kaufman. "Mexico-U.S. Relations: Big Initiatives Can Cause Big Problems." *Foreign Affairs*, (Winter, 1981-1982), pp. 379-392.

Salazar, Robert. "Asociación de Reclamantes vs. The United Mexican States," Denver, Colorado, 1981.

Saragoza, Alejandro, "Behind the Scenes: Media Ownership, Politics and Popular Culture in Mexico, 1930-1958," Chicano Studies, University of California at Berkeley. 1981.

Zazueta, Carlos H. "Mexicans in the U.S. and Mexico's Foreign Policy: Emerging Trends for the 1980's." Version Preliminar. July, 1980.

THE CHICANO ELITE IN CHICANO-MEXICANO RELATIONS

Armando Gutierrez

The relationship between Chicanos and Mexicanos begins at that historical juncture where Chicanos become a culturally distinct ethnic group. The relationship must be understood territorially as Chicanos are now concentrated in an area that was once Mexico. It must also be understood socially as the border region has never quite been a rigid demarcation line between the United States and Mexico; at least, not where Chicanos and Mexicanos are concerned. The shifting nationalities of the region have never impaired the constant and virtually uninterrupted back and forth flow of people and ideas.

There is ample evidence to demonstrate that Mexico has long concerned itself with its *Mexico de afuera*—Mexican peregrination in the United States and those U.S. citizens of Mexican descent, Chicanos. Scholars, among them Juan Gomez Quinones, Carlos Zazueta, and Francisco Balderrama[1] have demonstrated that Mexico has historically expended significant resources in defending the rights of this *Mexico de afuera*. When one considers the usually pliant relationship between the U.S. and Mexico, it is surprising how vigorous Mexico has been in its protest of the maltreatment of Chicanos and Mexicanos. This is particularly true from 1848 through to the end of World War II.

In fact, there is some evidence to indicate that until World War II, Mexico did not distinguish between Mexicanos and Chicanos on the strict basis of citizenship.[2] As the Mexican government, through its consulates, continually objected to the failure of the United States to protect the civil and human rights of Mexicans, it included Chicanos without distinction. For example, during the Sleepy Lagoon Case and the Zoot Suit Riots in Los Angeles, most of the known victims of legal injustice were Chicanos. Yet, the Mexican consulate vigorously involved itself in their defense.[3] More recently in 1978 President Jose Lopez Portillo lamented to President Jimmy Carter the lack of protections afforded Chicanos by the U.S. government.[4]

In discussing the relations between Chicanos and Mexicans in recent history, it is useful to distinguish the actors involved. First, we may identify the Mexican elite. Government officials and functionaries, as well as members of the intellectual community, are included in this group. There has been little unity of opinion among this elite group regarding whether such relations should in fact take place, and, if so, what direction the relations ought to take.

The Mexican population in general comprises the second group. These are Mexicans in Mexico and those in the U.S. It is at the general population level that most of the interaction between Chicanos and Mexicanos takes place. This contact stems from the constant flow of Mexicanos and Chicanos back and forth across the border and the residential segregation existing along the Southwestern region of the U.S.[5] This contact, nurtured by over a century of a virtually non-existent border, insures that interaction will continue regardless of what happens among officials and the elite group of actors.

There also exists now an emerging Chicano elite. This group is composed, principally, of Chicano elected and appointed officials, a group that is increasing rapidly and one that will certainly play an ever more important role in relations between the U.S., Mexico, and the Chicano community. The Chicano elite also includes representatives of organizations such as, the League of United Latin American Citizens (LULAC), the American G.I. Forum, the Mexican American Legal Defense and Education Fund (MALDEF), the Chicano intellectual community and Chicano representatives of the media. In recent years, these groups have gained an increased legitimacy as representatives of the Chicano community. Intellectuals, especially, have played an important role in the development of relations with Mexico. A number of Chicano newspaper and television journalists regularly cover Mexican issues along with issues pertinent to the Chicano community.[6] Indeed, before taking office, President-elect Miguel de la Madrid met with a group of Chicano media representatives. These individuals, because of their background and heritage, are important in defining and interpreting for the general population the limits and reaches of relations between Chicanos and Mexicanos.

The Chicano community in general, like its Mexican counterpart, is the focus of interaction between Chicanos and Mexicanos. Chicanos and Mexicans live side by side, attend schools together and work in the same industries. Furthermore, a recent study indicates that 62 percent of Chicanos in California have visited Mexico.[7] This demonstrates that the thrust of the interaction is not simply northward, but that Chicanos, for professional, commercial, and personal reasons, do take the interaction southward.

Finally, the government of the United States is an unremitting actor in the relations. Beyond the political and economic dominance of Mexico, part and parcel of U.S. hemispheric politics, U.S. officials have expressed in no uncertain terms that the U.S. government must be included in the developing relations between Chicanos and Mexicanos.[8]

This paper examines the role of the Chicano elite in the development of contact with the Mexican Presidency. It describes the motives of the various groups involved and examines how two factions within the elite competed with each other to represent Chicano interests to the Mexican President. The observations are drawn from the author's role as a participant, observer, and organizer of many of the meetings between the Chicano elite and representatives of the President of Mexico, Partido Revolutionario Institucional (PRI) officials, high-level bureaucrats, academics, and other representatives of Mexico's elite class.

THE ECHEVERRIA ADMINISTRATION (1970-1976)

Mexico began to take an active interest in the Chicano community during the presidency of Luis Echeverria Alvarez. There are several reasons for this renewal of interest. First, President Echeverria had a personal interest in the *Mexico de afuera*, and more specifically, Chicanos. Echeverria was intimately aware, as are all Mexicans, of the dubious appropriation of half of Mexico's territory by the United States. He was also aware of the subsequent maltreatment of those Mexicans who chose to remain in the ceded areas and accept U.S. citizenship.

Second, Echeverria also decided, early in his administration, to move Mexico in the direction of a more active foreign policy. This break with the isolation of the past had significant ramifications for Mexico and its relations with the United States. For Chicanos, this new direction paved an avenue for greater and more active relations.

Third, and perhaps most important, was Echeverria's desire to have Mexico assume the leadership of the Third World. Echeverria perceived Mexico to be on the verge of unprecedented economic expansion, an expansion that, coupled with Mexico's stable political apparatus, would have allowed it to become a model for the developing world. It was at this moment in history that the Chicano intellectual elite proposed that Chicanos were an "internal colony" and that, as such, they properly belonged within the Third World.[9]

Fourth, Echeverria came to his office with a tarnished image. While head of the Department of the Interior in the previous administration of Gustavo Diaz Ordaz, Mexican troops under his direction attacked student demonstrators at Tlatelolco in 1968, killing some 300 of the demonstrators. If he was to become the leader of the Third World, he would have to ameliorate the reputation which preceded him. To welcome Chicanos in Mexico and to offer aid to this oppressed group presented Echeverria with two opportunities. In the first instance, his support would not go unnoticed by the liberation movements who might be skeptical of him because of Tlatelolco. In the second instance, to provide aid to a dispossessed ethnic group within the borders of the U.S. would be an important act of defiance and it would signal Mexico's renewed confidence as a nation. This, too, would not go unnoticed by Third World nations who generally regard the U.S. as the source of underdevelopment woes.

Finally, there were reciprocal interests involved in the developing of a relationship between Chicanos and Mexicanos. Mexico, since the mid-19th century, has been at a severe disadvantage in its relations with the U.S. Chicanos offered the possibility of increased leverage for Mexico. How this leverage would operate and to what extent it would improve Mexico's position, is still unknown. However, in the early 1970s, the Chicano Movement had considerable potential in terms of influence. Whether that potential influence will be borne out by history is another matter; this potential, however, would not have been lost to the Echeverria administration.

As may be observed from the variety of actors involved in Chicano and Mexicano relations, along with the variety of motives underlying the participation of the actors, the nature of Chicano and Mexicano relations is quite complex. Surely, Mexico's involvement was not purely altruistic. However, Chicanos stood to make significant gains as well. There have been critics of the relationship, it should be noted, who have charged that Mexico actively and consciously manipulated Chicanos in the relations for the sole benefit of Mexico. This notion is rejected. The actors from the Chicano community were perceptive, skilled, and shrewd political players. That fact alone belies the charge as stated. The justification at the onset of the relations, as it remains still, is the conviction that it would benefit the Chicano community. The evidence supplied by the decade and more that the relationship has existed indicates that Chicanos indeed benefitted, especially, the elite.

With the expressed support of President Echeverria, a dialogue began to develop between representatives of the Mexican and Chicano communities. A conference on Chicanos was organized and took place in Mexico City in 1971. During the conference, President Echeverria met with Chicano leaders such as Reies Lopez Tijerina, leader of the land grant struggle in New Mexico; Jose Angel Gutierrez, founder of the Raza Unida Party; and noted Chicano film maker, Jesus Salvador Trevino.

The result of these meetings was a two-fold program of assistance for Chicanos to be funded by the Mexican government. Funding was made available for the production of two films with a strong Chicano content. The implied market for the production was a Mexican audience largely unaware of the condition of the *Mexico de afuera*. A further stipulation restricted the production to as much Chicano participation as possible in all facets of film making.

The second part of the program provided funding for the study of medicine at Mexican universities. An administrative unit, staffed by Chicanos, would recruit, screen, and award a number of medical scholarships each year to Chicano students who otherwise might be denied such an opportunity. An addendum to the program provided for the distribution of books and materials about Mexico to libraries throughout the southwestern U.S.

As modest as this initial program might appear, it is a landmark in relations between Chicanos and Mexicanos. The specifics of the aid program are secondary to the precedent and the tone they set. Most important of all, as will be shown later, it affected the internal politics of the Chicano elite and also affected the relation between the United States and Mexico in that it interposed Chicanos in the dialogue between the two countries.

The idea of interaction with Chicanos did not make significant inroads into the government and academic sectors of Mexico. Indeed, if many of Echeverria's bold initiatives bore an element of risk, relations with Chicanos were *terra incognita* altogether. There was no precedent for such efforts. Historically, Mexican intervention on behalf of Chicano interests was dictated by the conditions of a specific situation or individual. Moreover, Mexican policy toward its *Mexico de afuera* became increasingly modulated since the 1940s. As with most bureaucracies, to maintain the status quo is the norm. New and innovative policy is slow to wind its way through the resistance of habit and the reluctance to venture into uncharted territory.

In fairness to the Mexican elite, Chicanos were an unknown entity in the world of international diplomacy. There was no clearly identifiable pyramid of leadership with which to negotiate. The clamor of separate voices and divergent interests produced doubts as to whether such a relationship should be established. The apprehensions were serious enough to produce doubts as to the behavior of Chicanos in the protocol and decorum-conscious drawing rooms of international diplomacy.

Although the Echeverria Presidency was marked by changes in style and policy, the personnel in his administration were drawn largely from the old Mexican aristocracy and the ranks of the party loyal who made a career in government service. This Mexican elite view the working class of any nationality with disdain. Many of them were in strategic positions in relation to a dialogue with Chicanos and they strongly opposed interaction with *pochos*, a derisive term which, linguistically, has traditionally served, at the popular level, to distinguish between Chicanos and Mexicanos. They were reluctant to run the political risk of assuming liability in the event that Echeverria's overture became a fiasco. Such an encounter had all of the overtones of Russian roulette, considering that the Mexican political system, not unlike political systems in general, frequently rewards those who do not act rather than vice versa.

It is not surprising, then, that the principal leadership in the developing of relations between Chicanos and Mexicanos came not from a career politician or a government bureaucrat, but from a university professor, Dr. Jorge Bustamante. To be sure, the risks were still substantial, but Professor Bustamante could act without many of the political and social constraints which the task might otherwise impose.

Jorge Bustamante was an ideal choice to spearhead Echeverria's interest in the dialogue. He was familiar with the U.S., having received his Ph.D. in Sociology from the University of Notre Dame. Professor Bustamante had also conducted considerable research on Mexican immigration to the U.S. and in the process had become knowledgeable about the situation of Chicanos. Further he was personally acquainted with the leadership of various Chicano organizations. Equally important, Dr. Bustamante had lived in the U.S. during the 1960s and 1970s and had been able to observe first hand the development of the Chicano Movement.

The skepticism in Mexico, however, continued unabated. There remained a good deal of ambiguity as to what Mexico could achieve by such a relationship with what essentially amounts to a dispossessed group. The most often cited analogy was to the American Jewish community's influence on U.S. policy in the Middle East, and, to a lesser extent, the influence of Cuban Americans on policy towards the island nation. Whether Chicanos could muster the requisite political and economic forces to make the analogy apt was extremely problematic. Of course, with Mexico's help, the situation could conceivably improve.

One serious complication was the internal economic problems of Mexico. Mexico has one of the world's most unequal distributions of economic resources. For Mexico to provide aid for Chicanos, at whatever cost, would leave open the criticism that the administration was providing for non-citizens what it failed to provide for its citizens.

Further, Mexico has long maintained a foreign policy based on the principle of non-intervention. This policy maintains that each country and its people are sovereign, with the right to self-determination. According to Mexican philosophy, this right is absolute, extending even to the most disdainful forms of government. The development of a relationship with Chicanos had implications for this policy since Mexico would in effect be violating one of the tenets of its foreign policy by entering into compact with citizens of another country, a compact outside of routine diplomatic channels. Still, with the new directions in foreign policy, there was not yet a distinction between an activist policy and intervention. This latter point, coupled with Mexico's moral obligations to its *Mexico de afuera*, lent a considerable degree of legitimacy to the undertaking.

Another serious consideration was the reaction of the U.S. to the relationship. Although some observers posit the relationship between Mexico and the U.S. as one of interdependency, it is not a symmetrical relationship. Nearly three fifths of all Mexican trade is with the U.S. Conversely, less than five percent of U.S. trade is with Mexico. The vast majority of Mexico's foreign debt of more than $90 billion is owed to the U.S. There is also Mexico's dependence on tourism, drawn largely from the U.S., to bring in dollars and contribute to the economy.[10] The

51

significance of this dependency can hardly be overstated. This being the case, Mexico must be ever mindful of possible U.S. reactions to its policy decisions. Were the U.S. to accuse Mexico of meddling in its internal affairs, would the benefits to accrue be worth the risk of U.S. retaliation? In view of the U.S. policy of constant intervention in Latin American affairs, and in view of past U.S. military incursions into Mexico, the possibility of U.S. retaliation loomed heavily as the actors in the Mexican side of the dialogue moved forward.

The foregoing illustrate an atmosphere of apprehension as the establishment of a relationship between Chicanos and Mexicanos developed. The first, tentative, steps were nevertheless taken during the waning days of the Echeverria Administration. The general ambience, though still cautious was bolstered by the success of the initial contacts. As the election campaign of 1976 approached, the relationship moved to another level.

THE LOPEZ-PORTILLO ADMINISTRATION (1976-1982)

Following the election of Jose Lopez-Portillo, meetings were held with several Chicano groups. The meetings were designed to continue the relationship previously established and to acquaint the president-elect with the hopes, needs, and aspirations of Chicanos. Procedurally, the meetings were important because, by this point, Chicanos were received along with other interest groups in Mexico.

Upon assuming the presidency in December, 1976, Lopez-Portillo approved the continuation and expansion of the Chicano scholarship program instituted under Echeverria. The President approved fifty scholarships per year for the duration of his six-year term at a cost of approximately $12 million. The restrictions to medicine were lifted to include other fields of study. This program was administered by people associated with the Raza Unida Party, notably, Jose Angel Gutierrez.

Midway through his administration, and at the initiative of Jose Angel Gutierrez, Lopez-Portillo approved an additional scholarship program for Chicanos. Under this new program, university instructors and graduate students in Chicano and Mexican studies would attend the Colegio de Mexico in Mexico City for intensive study in Mexican politics, economics, history, and social problems. This scholarship program was administered by the Mexican American Studies Program at the University of Houston.

Lamentably, other than the continued and new scholarship programs, little of substance occurred during the Lopez-Portillo Administration to further enhance the relationship between Chicanos and Mexicanos. President Lopez-Portillo did meet periodically with the leadership of several Chicano groups but the result of those meetings did not change the caution of the previous administration.

CHICANO REACTIONS

Interestingly, during the early stages of the development of the relationship between Chicanos and Mexicanos, many Chicanos were not particularly interested in a dialogue with Mexico. In particular, the more moderate to conservative leaders, such as those representing LULAC and the American G.I. Forum, not only were not interested but ridiculed advocates of such a relationship. Much of the Chicano leadership looked to traditional avenues for civil rights remedies. Chicanos, they argued, as U.S. citizens, should look to Washington and their respective state capitals for assistance in social change. There was nothing to gain by working with Mexico. Not until Eduardo Morga assumed the Presidency of LULAC in 1976 did this organization participate in the meetings with the President of Mexico. Even then, Morga had difficulty in obtaining support from his membership and in recruiting the leadership of other moderate Chicano organizations.

The inception of the scholarship program did more than anything to change the attitudes of the moderate and conservative organizations. These organizations have stressed the importance of education as the key to social mobility for Chicanos. In fact, many of the organizations, such as LULAC, have their own scholarship programs through which they encourage Chicanos to attend college. The first concrete results of the developing relationship were consistent with their own objectives. That the scholarship program was organized and managed by leaders whom they perceived as radical spurred the moderates to insert themselves into the relationship. This occurred during the time when the divisions among the Chicano national leadership were becoming pronounced.

For example, the defense of the Mexican undocumented worker and the challenge of Immigration and Naturalization Service (INS) policy began as an issue of the Chicano left. The Raza Unida Party, the Crusade for Justice, and the Centro de Accion Social Autonoma (CASA), among others, called attention to the alarmist trend developing in the U.S. toward Mexican immigration. The attenuation of U.S. immigration policy is largely due to the efforts of these groups. Initially, the moderate organizations were not interested in immigration from Mexico beyond the sporadic sponsoring of citizenship classes. However, as the general Chicano community responded to the issue, moderate groups began to adopt more progressive stances.

The increased participation of conservatives and moderates forced upon them a realization of the interconnectedness of Chicanos and Mexicanos. From a political standpoint, the moderates began to claim that if Chicanos defended undocumented workers and by extension helped the Mexican government, then Chicanos would be owed a debt which ought to be collected. In order to collect, the moderates would have to gain access to the Mexican government and to do so, they would have to ask individuals and organizations which they defined as radical to intercede on their behalf, or, they would have to shun them aside. In fact, they managed to do both.

The first organizers of the relationship between Chicanos and Mexicanos initially glossed over the ideological divisions among the different Chicano groups. Instead, they portrayed Chicanos as a group of some fifteen million people who shared a common history, culture, and language and who were largely of similar socio-economic standing. More importantly, they asserted that Chicanos were an organized and unified political group with the potential for significantly affecting regional and national politics in the U.S.

The intent was not to mislead. There was and continues to be a shared desire to improve the lot of Chicanos, but differences exist around philosophies and strategies. The temperament and personalities involved contributed to the differences. The long range vision of the initial organizers made it necessary to convince their contacts in Mexico that it was worthwhile to commit Mexico to a relationship with Chicanos. They argued that Chicanos could in fact be galvanized into providing a substantial payoff for Mexico because they were united. To present an unnecessarily complicated description of Chicano factionalism, would exacerbate an already apprehensive attitude in Mexico. Thus, it followed naturally that when the moderate and conservative organizations petitioned, they received participation in the relationship.

THE RISE TO PROMINENCE OF CHICANO MODERATES

Thus, the moderates gained access to the Mexican government at the invitation of groups which the moderates perceived as radical. As Lopez-Portillo began to have periodic meetings with Chicanos, more representatives of the moderate organizations accepted the invitations to attend. Through their own initiatives, they began to develop contacts with Mexican government functionaries, bureaucrats and politicians. Soon, they began to attempt to organize meetings with President Lopez-Portillo on their own and to determine the attendance list. The moderates argued that it was they who represented the majority of Chicanos and that they should legitimately be entitled to maintain the liaison between Chicanos and Mexicanos. They criticized the initial organizers, labelling them as communists and militants with no discernible constituency in the Chicano community.

The moderates claims to leadership were not without foundation. During this period, organizations such as LULAC, the American G.I. Forum, and MALDEF, had received considerable attention from the U.S. government and, in particular, from the U.S. media. This gave credence to their claims. The moderates' criticism of the radicals did not come without costs, though. Mexican officials began to seriously reconsider with whom they would negotiate and they cooled to the relationship.

Perhaps most damaging was the fracture of unity so laboriously articulated by the initial organizers. The criticisms exposed by the moderates made clear that Chicanos were a fragmented group with serious internal divisions and little or no unity of purpose. As might be expected, once the illusion of group harmony and cohesiveness was shattered the relationship between Chicanos and Mexicanos began to change.

The first change to occur involved the liaison between the Mexican government and Chicanos. Since the origin of the relationship in the Echeverria Administration and through the first half of the Lopez-Portillo presidency, Dr. Jorge Bustamante had been in charge of coordinating relations on the Mexican side. Dr. Jose Angel Gutierrez, founder of the Raza Unida Party and one of the initial organizers, was coordinator on the U.S. side for Chicanos. Although the mechanisms used by Bustamante and Gutierrez were largely informal and voluntary, it was nevertheless very productive.

In 1979, however, Lic. Guido Belsasso, a career bureaucrat, was given responsibility for Chicano-Mexicano relations. The appointment represented a return to the normal pattern of Mexican politics whereby such assignments are routinely handed to career bureaucrats as a reward for loyal service. The *ad hoc* nature of the relationship and the presence of an individual in the form of Bustamante with no official ties to the ruling party or to the government were both anomalies to normal routine.

The second change to occur was to have a more significant effect on Chicano-Mexicano relations. Toward the end of 1979, President Lopez-Portillo announced the creation of *La Comision Mixta de Enlace*. This commission, under the Secretario de Trabajo, was to be the formal structure through which Chicano-Mexicano relations were to be conducted.

The Commission, as proposed by the LULAC leadership, was composed as follows: LULAC, Project SER, American G.I. Forum, MALDEF, National Association of Farmworker Organizations (NAFO), Mexican American Women's National Association (MANA), National IMAGE, National Hispanic Forum, National Council of La Raza, and a Puerto Rican organization (ASPIRA). The Executive Council of La Comision consisted of Ruben Bonilla, national president of LULAC, Jose Cano, national president of the American G.I. Forum and Vilma Martinez, Executive Director, MALDEF. None of the initial organizers were included. Shortly after its founding, *La Comision* lapsed into a largely ceremonial relationship, and, thus, a new and more traditional phase of Chicano-Mexican relations began.

THE DECLINE OF THE LEFT

The initial organizers of contact with Mexico were leaders of organizations to the left of center in political ideology. Their decreasing influence in Chicano-Mexicano relations was not entirely the work of the moderates but was also due in part to events occurring internally within the Chicano political left. The case of Jose Angel Gutierrez is instructive. During the nascent stage of the Chicano Movement, Gutierrez occupied the most prominent role on the Chicano political scene. He was seen as an ideologue, a shrewd strategist, and an extraordinarily charismatic figure. His electoral successes with the Raza Unida Party in Zavala County in Texas, afforded him a base from which to operate and also provided the basis for his legitimacy as a Chicano leader. Under the banner of the Raza Unida Party, Gutierrez and a coalition of Chicanos engineered a clean sweep of elective offices in Zavala County. Gutierrez was elected County Judge. Armed with the prestige of an elected office, Gutierrez had little difficulty in making contact with Mexico.

However, the contacts and the leaders and organizations he recruited came with attendant costs. He spent a great deal of time in Mexico and elsewhere in the U.S. trying to develop a national constituency. His frequent absences left him open to criticism as to his limited commitment to Crystal City and South Texas. Gutierrez also has a strong personality and he seldom minces words. His stridency tended to create political enemies, both within the left and among the moderates. Gutierrez, for example, was criticized by the left for negotiating with the Partido Revolucionario Institucional (PRI). Early on in the relationship, the memory of Echeverria's complicity in the Tlatelolco massacre was vivid and remained a point of contention within the Chicano left. The Raza Unida Party was also attacked by the left as lacking a clear ideology, of being a cultural nationalist organization and of creating the illusion that change could be effected through the electoral process.

The Raza Unida Party also produced a deep bitterness among moderates who were members of the Democratic Party. Among Chicano Democrats, Raza Unida caused far more damage than the Republican Party because it siphoned off traditional Chicano support for the Democratic Party. Conversely, Gutierrez reserved his harshest criticism for Chicano Democrats who, he charged, did little to improve the condition of the Chicano community.

Jose Angel Gutierrez similarly inspired important detractors in Mexico. His brashness and self-confidence was interpreted by Mexicans as an arrogant, distinctly American trait. Gutierrez' direct, no-nonsense style, conflicted with the deferential air adopted as a formal style within Mexican institutions.

Also, toward the end of the Echeverria Administration, the Raza Unida Party had begun to disintegrate as a regional, state, and national political force in the Chicano community. Similarly, other progressive organizations such as the Crusade for Justice began to concentrate on local issues in Denver, Colorado and the land grant struggle of New Mexico began to wane as well. In Zavala County, the coalition brought together by Gutierrez began to oppose him and to mount serious opposition to his programs.

With left of center groups losing their influence in the general Chicano community, the stage was thus set for a change in the relations between Mexico and Chicanos. As the left organizations declined, the void was filled by moderate organizations which had been maneuvering themselves into position.

THE CAMPAIGN OF MIGUEL DE LA MADRID (1982)

With the political leadership of the initial organizers in disarray, the moderates unsure of their position, and the impending end of the Lopez-Portillo Administration, the relations with Mexico again faced an uncertain future. There was no doubt that new actors were waiting in the wings. Miguel de la Madrid was largely an unknown personality in Chicano political circles. His principal exposure to Chicanos had occurred in 1979 and 1980 when he visited San Antonio and Los Angeles as an official representative of Lopez-Portillo to the Fiestas Patrias celebrations.

Upon receiving the PRI nomination for the presidency, de la Madrid appointed Bernardo Sepulveda as his Foreign Minister. Sepulveda, who had been at the Colegio de Mexico with Jorge Bustamante, asked his colleague to draft a plan for a meeting between de la Madrid and Chicanos. The plan submitted to Sepulveda called for a series of three meetings. Part of the plan included a provision for the appointment of a Chicano to serve as an advisor to the campaign on Chicano affairs. The approval of this portion of the plan cleared the way for a more extensive interaction.

The first meeting included a group of leaders from Chicano social and political organizations. Conspicuously absent were representatives from any of the organizations of the left. The purpose of the initial meeting was exploratory. It was designed to acquaint the candidate with prominent Chicano actors in the relationship. It also provided an opportunity for the candidate to explain some basic principles of Mexican politics and to advance an outline of his plans for the country.

There was concern on the Mexican side that the Chicanos who had previously interacted with Mexico had a very limited understanding of the intricacies of the Mexican political system. Further, this limitation often interfered with the formation of a more productive relationship. The intention was to provide Chicanos with the limits and range of the relationship given the realities of Mexican politics.

The meeting was held on March 3, 1983. Referring to earlier interaction with Chicanos, de la Madrid stated, ". . . this meeting . . . should above all else be understood as a reaffirmation of the willingness of the Partido Revolucionario Institucional and its candidate to the Presidency of Mexico, to fortify, expand and systematize these linkages that, having as their base history and sentiment, can evolve into forms of cooperation even more dynamic and positive."[11]

Later in the campaign, de la Madrid held a second meeting, this time with a group of Chicano intellectuals, in Juarez, Mexico. This group made a series of presentations covering issues pertinent to the Chicano community. Among the topics were bilingual education, the status of Chicano Studies programs in U.S. universities, the defense of undocumented workers and their children by Chicanos, the scholarship programs funded by Mexico, women's issues, and legal efforts to erase the lingering effects of discrimination.

In his presentation, candidate de la Madrid recognized the complexity of the relationship. ". . . one manner of defending the rights of these communities (Chicano and Mexicano) is to reaffirm their cultural identity and the solidarity produced within these communities because such a reaffirmation gives both of us more leverage in the process of social and political negotiation within the United States of America."[12] De la Madrid thus made a significant admission regarding the importance of the emerging political, social and economic power of the Chicano community. It also indicated that increased Chicano strength can translate into added leverage for Mexico in its relations with the U.S.

The third and final meetings with de la Madrid took place following his election to the Presidency of Mexico. The meeting occurred immediately after the new President met with Ronald Reagan, President of the United States, in San Diego, California. Once again, he met with Chicano scholars hastily brought together when the scheduled meetings with Chicano journalists was postponed. This last meeting produced concrete results, with de la Madrid pledging his support for the continuation of the existing scholarship programs. He further indicated that the possibilities were not in the least limited. He added, "there must surely be other specific programs that by means of organization and collaborative efforts between the government of Mexico and the Mexican American community . . . can be realized."[13] President de la Madrid signalled in unequivocal terms his willingness to maintain not only the symbolic and ceremonial aspects of the relationship between Chicanos and Mexico, but his desire to move on to more substantive interaction.

CONCLUSION

President Miguel de la Madrid's affirmation of the relationship between Chicanos and Mexico is a recognition of the major changes occurring within the general Chicano community which are destined to become a significant factor in the relationship. Three, in particular, should be noted.

First, are the demographic trends among Chicanos. The Chicano population is the fastest growing minority group in the U.S. Between 1970 and 1980, the Spanish-speaking population in the U.S. grew by some 61 percent to a total of 15 million. This compares with a 17.3 percent growth rate for Blacks and 10 percent for the total population. Approximately two-thirds of the Spanish-speaking population is concentrated in the states of California, New Mexico, Arizona, Florida, and Texas. The U.S., in fact, is now the fourth largest Spanish-speaking nation in the Western Hemisphere. To state the obvious, Chicanos, by virtue of their increasing numbers, must be reckoned with in the internal and external politics of the U.S.

Second, Chicanos are already an important political bloc, especially in those states which share a border with Mexico. Chicanos, for example, form key voting blocs in strategic states, such as California and Texas. The Democratic National Convention had more than 500 Spanish-surname delegates to its 1980 meetings.

President Jimmy Carter appointed Leonel Castillo as Director of the Immigration and Naturalization Service and Julian Nava as Ambassador to Mexico. Carter also actively solicited Hispanic support for the Panama Canal Treaty ratification. In October, 1979, the State Department sponsored a conference on foreign affairs for 200 Hispanic political, academic, and business figures. These examples indicate that Chicanos are becoming a force in U.S. domestic and foreign policy.

Third, and finally, the Chicano population is having a dramatic impact in the economic sphere. Chicanos are on the rise as entrepreneurs and as consumers. Between 1972 and 1977, the number of Hispanic-owned firms increased by 53 percent and their total receipts grew by 75 percent. If the current growth rate is maintained, there will be some 1 million Hispanic firms by the year 2000 with receipts in excess of $150 billion. In 1977 there were over 440 Hispanic-owned firms with annual revenues of $1 million or more. There are 58 Spanish-language newspapers and magazines in the U.S., and there are 450 radio and television stations with full or part-time Spanish-language broadcasting.

It is not possible to make any but the most guarded predictions for the future of Chicano and Mexicano relations. The development of the Chicano community, independent of Mexico, will improve its negotiating position in the relationship. Further, the Chicano community has much to offer to the U.S. with respect to foreign policy in Latin America. There is little question then that, specifics aside, the future of the Chicano community is as bright as it is impressive.

FOOTNOTES

1. See, for example: Juan Gomez-Quinones, "Notes on an Interpretation of the Relations Between the Mexican Community in the United States and Mexico"; Carlos H. Zazueta, "Mexican Political Actors in the United States and Mexico: Historical and Political Contexts of a Dialogue Renewed." in Carlos Vasquez and Manual Garcia Y Griego (editors), *Mexican-U.S. Relations Conflict and Convergence* (UCLA Chicano Studies Research Center Publications and UCLA Latin American Center Publications, University of California, Los Angeles, 1983); Francisco Balderrama, *In Defense of La Raza*, (Tuscon, Arizona, University of Arizona Press, 1982).
2. Juan Gomez-Quinones. op. cit.
3. Rodolfo Acuna, *Occupied America* (New York, Harper and Row, 1981).
4. Jose Angel Gutierrez, "Chicanos and the Mexican President," Paper presented at U.S.-Mexico Relations Conference, University of California at Los Angeles, March, 1982.
5. Marc Matre & Tatcho Mindiola, Jr., "Residential Segregation in Southwestern Metropolitan Areas: 1970, *Sociological Focus*, 14, January 1981, pgs. 15-31.
6. For example: Frank del Olmo, *Los Angeles Times*, Felipe Garcia, *Arizona Daily Star*, Elias Castillo, *San Jose Mercury* and Juan Palomo, *Houston Post*.
7. Juan Gomez-Quinones. op. cit.
8. Private conversation with Jorge Bustamante, Professor of Sociology, Colegio de Mexico, Mexico City, March 1983.
9. Tomas Almaguer, "Toward the Study of Chicano Colonialism," *Aztlan*, Vol. 2, No. 1, Spring 1971, pgs. 7-20. Mario Barrera, Carlos Munoz, Charles Ornelas, "The Barrio as Internal Colony," in Harlan Hahn (ed.) *Urban Affairs Annual Review*, Vol. 6, 1972.
10. Dennis Drabelle, "Mexico Explored: Our Neighbor's Pain and Politics," *USA Today*, March 8, 1985, pg. 3D.
11. Speech entitled, "Discurso Pronunciado Por el Lic. Miguel de la Madrid Hurtado Ante Dirigentes Politicos Chicanos el 3 de marza de 1982," Mexico City, Mexico, D.F., page 4, Author's personal copy.
12. Speech entitled, "Discurso Pronunciado Por el Lic. Miguel de La Madrid Hurtado Ante Intelectuales Chicanos, el 12 abril de 1982, Cd. Juarez, Chih., page 19. Author's personal copy.
13. Speech entitled, "Discurso Pronunciado Por el Lic. Miguel de la Madrid Hurtado Ante Representantes de la Comunidad Chicana, el 9 octubre de 1982, San Diego, California, page 20. Author's personal copy.

THE IMPACT OF IMMIGRATION IN THE ETHNIC ENTERPRISE

Gilbert Cardenas

During the past ten years, Mexican immigration, undocumented immigration in particular, has come under severe attack from a small yet vocal sector of American society. The alarm over undocumented migration is based upon an uneasy perception that undocumented migration is on the increase and that it is out of control. This reaction is further extended to include legal immigration.

Opponents to Mexican immigration argue that it causes a severe drain on the economy and that it is disrupting the population balance of American society. They argue that immigration adversely affects labor markets by depressing wage rates thereby causing higher levels of unemployment. They argue further that immigrants, and undocumented immigrants in particular, drain the tax coffers by using publicly supported health services disproportionately to their contribution.

The general alarm over immigration, specifically the reaction to undocumented immigrants, has generated considerable attention within the academic research community. In the seven to eight years since the inception of the negative reaction, the academic research community has begun to produce data which contradict most of the assumptions concerning immigration. Researchers, for example, have begun to specify a more probable range for the number of undocumented migrants in the United States at any given time. Commissioner Leonard Chapman of the Immigration and Naturalization Service and Congressman Peter Rodino estimated a range of twelve to eighteen million immigrants in the U.S. illegally (Cardenas, 1976). Researchers now place this figure at three to four million (Warren and Passel, 1984).

Much of the research on the use of publicly supported services has been funded by government agencies. This empirical research suggests the following concerning undocumented migrants: (1) they use few publicly supported services or benefits programs, (2) they pay far more than they receive in tax-supported programs, and (3) they subsidize the tax system.

The research concerning the effects of immigration on the labor market is far more problematic, yet no study to date has produced results that establish a direct test of adverse labor effects. The empirical research on this question is ambiguous, yet researchers seem to be more disposed to specify particular labor markets rather than to generalize to the entire economy as they once were.

One of the justifications for opposing immigration is the claim that it hurts minorities most. Thus they argue that restrictive immigration measures would benefit minorities. Yet, as we have noted in another paper, the most ardent proponents of a restrictive immigration policy have come primarily from outside of the minority community. One would expect, for example, that Chicanos would be the most insistent and vocal opponents to Mexican immigration. Yet, the Chicano community, including national organizations, politicians, academics, unions, etc., have generally reacted in a positive and supportive way.

In spite of the recent findings produced by academic researchers and public officials, some scholars continue to argue that immigration, especially undocumented immigration, negatively affects the economy and they continue to postulate that minorities are hurt the most (Briggs, 1978). Moreover, according to the some of the arguments, minorities stand to lose the most were immigration not drastically curtailed.

Current research has revealed that Mexican immigration has a far more positive impact on the Chicano community. Mexican immigrants and Chicanos have a symbiotic relationship which tends to benefit both groups when they exist in the same residential neighborhoods and community areas.

Were one to emphasize the negative effects of immigration in specific labor markets in specific sectors of the economy and in specific localities, one would still be hard-pressed to conclude that this immigration produces a net negative effect. This is due in large measure to the operation of the ethnic economy. A better approach with which to assess these effects would be a focus on the overall impact that immigration has on the ethnic economy and the various sub-systems of ethnic enclaves.[1]

This conception would include analyzing the function of ethnic-specific labor markets and their broader articulation in non-ethnic-specific labor markets, i.e., the role and function of Mexican workers in and outside of the ethnic enclave. Immigrant workers and their families benefit the ethnic enclave in definite and measurable ways. Similarly, the ethnic enclave benefits immigrants by providing maintenance and employment functions and an environment of socio-cultural support.

The overall vitality of the ethnic enclave is strengthened rather than debilitated by immigrants. Moreover, the social mobility of many middle class Chicanos is highly dependent on the presence of immigrants. Minorities, e.g., Chicanos, the commercial sector, the social mobile class and the community at large is probably more adversely affected when immigration is curtailed. For example, the periodic raids by the INS have a disruptive effect on the commercial districts of Chicano enclaves. The "downtown" establishments are virtually deserted during INS round-up periods. This has a depressing effects on ethnic businesses and effects middle class Chicanos who provide services to the Mexican immigrant population. Thus, compared to other groups, ethnics are directly affected by the intimidation resulting from periodic or long-term curtailment of immigration.

The competitive ability of ethnic entrepreneurs depends on their relative ability to corner the ethnic immigration market. This may be as important as their relative success in borrowing start-up capital or establishing or expanding their businesses. Similarly, the very survival of many small ethnic enterprises, and the jobs of their Chicano employees, may depend upon immigrant trade as much as upon native-born ethnic clientele. In summary, a more useful analysis of the economic interrelations between immigrants and minorities would include the interdependencies between labor markets and product markets.

ETHNIC ECONOMY: SOME WORKING DEFINITIONS

Based upon the definitions of ethnicity cited previously we will define the ethnic enclave within a boundary-maintenance framework. This suggests that an ethnic economy is situated and operational within a specific residential-commercial area where the majority of merchants and residents are ethnically similar. Ethnic economy is the sum of all economic activities in an ethnically specific territory.

There are various levels to the ethnic economy. These levels include formal and informal economic activity. The formal is divided into two main sectors, the primary and the secondary. As in all other economies, there are legal and illegal activities in the formal ethnic economy. Informal economic activities are those outside of state regulation and, in general, are not part of the tax system.

An ethnic enterprise is a commercial establishment that is distinguished from others primarily by the ethnicity of the owner, proprietor or manager; the ethnicity of its employees (labor force), the ethnicity of its clientele and by the ethnicity of other commercial establishments in the area, i.e., commercial or residential blocks. This definition offers a number of possibilities in the types of ethnic enterprises which make up the ethnic economy. The idealized form could be expressed in the following manner:

$$E \doteq O_e \doteq P_e \doteq M_e \doteq L_e \doteq C_e \doteq B_e$$

Where E=ethnic economy; O=owners; P=proprietors; M=managers; L=labor force, employees; C=clientele; and B=business establishments in a specific commercial or residential area, and e=ethnic.

Variations in the types of ethnic economies or mixed forms of ethnic economies could be expressed in any number of combinations where the proportions would change on any of the factors on the right side of the expression:

$$O_e \tilde{\neq} P_e \tilde{\neq} M_e \tilde{\neq} L_e \tilde{\neq} C_e \tilde{\neq} B_e$$

Ethnic-specific labor markets are those labor markets which draw upon an ethnic-specific labor force and ethnic-specific product markets are those product markets which rely on ethnic-specific targeting of its products and services.

Before proceeding any further, it may be useful to examine briefly the historical experience of the ethnic economy in the United States. It is important to understand the general context of an ethnic economy before one can focus attention upon the role, function and impact of Mexican immigration and its implications in the economy.

THE ETHNIC ENTERPRISE: AN HISTORICAL EXPERIENCE

It would be a questionable activity to assume that the experience of ethnic enterprises has been monolithic and one-dimensional. There are probably as many variations as there are major ethnic groups. A review of certain aspects of the experience of ethnic enterprise should reveal some of the distinctive characteristics and variations.

A common and widely accepted explanation for the differences of experience in the economic activity of Jews, Asians and Blacks rests with variations of discriminatory practices. Jews, for example, were forced into commercial pursuits in Europe and in the United States because they were excluded from land ownership and membership in skilled worker guilds and unions. Joe Feagin argues that Jews were limited to the risky or marginal tasks that developing economies require due to intentionally anti-Jewish discrimination (Feagin, 1978: 165).

Observers of the American scene, such as Carey McWilliams, have long noted the discrimination factor as an integral part of the ethnic economy. "The quickest way to define the position that Jews occupy in the American economy is to mark off the fields in which Jewish participation is non-existent or of negligible importance" (McWilliams, 1948:142).

Jewish enterpreneurs turned to their own communities and developed ethnic-based commercial activity:

> The marginal, risky nature of their enterprises, as well as outside hostility, fostered the growth of an ethnic economy, where Jews would turn to other Jews for economic aid, whenever possible, in order to maintain and sustain their economic enterprise and their communities (Feagin, 1978:165).

McWilliams characterized Jewish businesses as marginal:

> General speaking, the businesses in which are concentrated are those in which a large risk-factor is involved; businesses peripheral to the economy; businesses originally regarded as unimportant; new industries and businesses which have traditionally carried a certain element of social stigma, such, for example, as the amusement industry and the liquor industry. Not being able to penetrate the key control industries, Jews have been compelled to occupy the interstitial, the marginal, positions in the American economy. In short, it is the quantitative rather than the qualitative aspect of their participation in industry and finance that most graphically delineates their position (McWilliams, 1948:148).

Ivan Light, in his book, *Ethnic Enterprise in America* (1972) argues that Chinese and Japanese entrepreneurship in the United States began as a response to discriminatory structures which precluded wage or salary employment above the menial level (Light, 1972:10). This variation of discrimination theory as applied to the formation of ethnic enterprise was discussed in an earlier publication by Mabel Newcomer. She concludes that foreign-born entrepreneurs find relatively better income and status rewards in self-employment than do native-born persons who have options and hence more advantages in the labor market.

> The persistent overrepresentation of the foreign born in businesses is not a testimony to the entrepreneurial drive of the foreign-born, nor an insidious commentary upon the lethargy of native-born Americans. Compared to the native-born, the foreign-born have received less schooling and hold less impressive educational credentials. They possess fewer high-priced salable skills. They experience discrimination because of their accents and ethnicity. Hence,

the foreign-born find in self-employment relatively better income and status rewards than do native-born persons who have advantages in the labour market (Newcomer, 1961:478).

Ivan Light's study of ethnic enterprise advances a consumer-demand theory to explain the maintenance of ethnic enterprise. Light argues that foreign-born people have special consumer demands which cannot be satisfied by existing businesses.

Since the immigrants spoke little English and had their own ethnic cultures, they needed stores to supply them with ethnic foods and other services (Light, 1972:11).

There are, of course, consumer demands provided for by ethnic entrepreneurs which are not different from the consumer demands of other groups. There are, too, standard consumer demands for which they provide that are quite different from those of non-ethnic consumers. Ethnic entrepreneurs cater to the exotic tastes of their clientele. Ethnic entrepreneurs are at an advantage to satisfy these three types of consumer demands because of their location within the ethnic enclave, their language affinity with their clientele, and the supply of ethnic-specific products. The ethnic-specific consumer patterns have a beneficial effect on ethnic enterprise.

Light describes a marked tendency among immigrant Chinese and Japanese small businessmen to depend, initially, on an exclusive ethnic clientele. Only later do these businesses expand to a more general trade (Light, 1972:14). Light is quick to point out that the ethnic consumer demand theory alone is inadequate to explain the full range of ethnic enterprise activity. He argues that Asian retail merchants have extensive trade with non-Asians. In part, the success of Chinese and Japanese merchants is a function of a culturally derived basis of economic organization.

The vitality of ethnic enterprise is partially due to entrepreneurial segregation, the protective commercial monopoly formally enjoyed by what Theodore Cross calls, the "ghetto service business" (Cross, 1969:213). This protection previously enjoyed by ghetto businessmen, according to Cross, has produced new forms of white competition for Black patrons. The new white competition for Black business has caused (1) the total number of Black-owned business to decrease by 20 percent between 1950 and 1960, (2) a severe reduction in the growth rate of Black-owned insurance companies, (3) a dramatic increase in the failure of Black service establishments, such as funeral parlors and nursing homes, dry cleaners, grocery stores, and hotels (Cross, 1969:213).

McWilliams argues that Jews were systematically excluded from dominant businesses and industries, yet pointed out that certain cultural and sociological factors have also been influential in bringing about the concentration of their economic endeavor. Cross suggests that the Black economy, that is the ghetto market, is a poor economy with drives similar to those of the main economy. He warns, however, that those drives are weaker than of those of the dominant economy.

Historical Role and Function of Immigrants in the Ethnic Economy

Immigration from Mexico is not a recent phenomenon. Immigration from Mexico has been steady since the turn of the century with dramatic influxes in the 1920s and 1970s. The steady pace of immigration, the boom periods notwithstanding, has had a continuous effect on ethnic economy. It is this aspect of Mexican immigration that distinguishes it from the experience of other immigrant groups. Herein lie the major differences in the role and function of Mexican immigrants in the ethnic economy.

Mexican immigrants have tended to settle in Chicano neighborhoods. As they maintain residences in these generally enclosed neighborhoods, their consumer and service needs are provided for within these circumscribed areas. Unlike the experience of other immigrant groups, however, the Mexican ethnic economy did not begin with nor was it entirely shaped by immigration or post-immigration activity.

One of the unique aspects of the ethnic economy is its dependence upon an extraordinarily high number of undocumented immigrants. The legal status of the immigration population is an important factor in the way that ethnic population functions in the ethnic economy. The cyclical nature of undocumented migration, with the workers moving between residence in Mexico and labor markets in the United States, has evolved into a permanent feature of an ethnic economy. In fact, it has become a quasi-institutional feature of it.

Thus, the role and function of the Mexican immigrant in an ethnic economy may be shaped by the continuous nature of his migration and by the composition and circulation of the immigrant population. Yet, despite the importance of these distinctive features of Mexican immigration, there are a number of similarities in the way all immigrants affect an ethnic economy. For example, an ethnic economy functions to provide:

1) a natural social mechanism for receiving new immigrant workers and an enabling mechanism for immigrants who seek to exit the ethnic enclave;

2) opportunities for work and self-employment training for Mexican workers;

3) a social setting for informal networking in the job search;

4) a social setting for reducing the cost of living;

5) a natural and powerful maintenance and integrative mechanism for Mexican workers.

The above may be perceived as benefits accruing to Mexican workers.

The Consumer demands of Immigrant Workers and an Ethnic Economy

In a recent paper, Cardenas, de la Garza and Hansen (1982) argued that the consumer patterns of Mexican workers directly benefit the Chicano community because their consumption (rent, food, clothing, services) is almost entirely limited to the Chicano community. This assumes that, of course, a majority of Mexican immigrant workers reside in Chicano communities as suggested by David North and Miriam Houston (1976). It, therefore, may be expected that:

1) the consumer demands of the immigrant population may be unique and may be satisfied only by ethnic entrepreneuers;

2) the consumer demands of immigrant workers may be in part similar to the consumer demands of non-immigrant ethnics and mainly satisfied by ethnic entrepreneurs;

3) the consumer demands of immigrant workers may be no different from the consumer demands of the general population and thus may be satisfied by both ethnic and non-ethnic entrepreneurs;

4) the unique, ethnic-specific and general consumer demands of the immigrant population contribute to the vitality of the ethnic economy and stimulates the vitality of the ethnic enclave;

5) the consumer demands of the immigrant population represent one component factor in the competitive advantage that ethnic entrepreneurs have and may be a major contributing factor in the profitability of the business.

Immigration Labor and the Mexican Ethnic Economy

The trade of immigrant workers tends to increase the profitability of marginal and non-marginal ethnic enterprises alike. The attractiveness of ethnic products and services for immigrant workers in the ethnic enclave may be due to lower prices offered by ethnic entrepreneurs for such goods and services. The lower prices may be the result of production costs unique to ethnic economic organization and the availability and use of labor that requires or prefers language proficiency in Spanish. These skills are routinely found in ethnic enclaves and may be functionally useful to ethnic entrepreneurs and Mexican workers alike. Yet, these same skills may not be as readily available, useful, or desirable outside the ethnic enclave.

The attractiveness of ethnic goods and services may be ethnic-specific initially. However, over a period of time, these products and services may become attractive to non-ethnic consumers, e.g., restaurants. This is similar to the expanded-clientele pattern described by Light for Asian businesses.

It does not follow that ethnic businesses are directly or necessarily in competition with non-ethnic businesses. In general, it is the limited availability of ethnic goods and services outside of the ethnic enclave which gives rise to ethnic-specific businesses within the ethnic enclave. In this respect, ethnic businesses may be viewed as complementary to the existing main economy.

Among the advantages which immigrant workers provide is their geographic mobility. Their availability for seasonal work particularly among single males, and their ability to change residence are assets which increase their competitive standing in secondary labor markets. Mexican workers often enjoy a distinct competitive advantage at entry-level jobs in secondary labor markets because of their previous employment histories, work experience, skills, and commitment to work. Thus, their employment behavior may be related as much to their competitive advantage in entry-level jobs in secondary labor markets as it is to their relative disadvantage in the illegal status of their immigration if they do not have proper documentation. It is an oversimplification of major proportions to assume that undocumented workers work harder for less wages simply because they are afraid of being caught.

General Benefits from the Presence of Immigrant Workers and Their Families in Economic Activities

The preceding discussion attempted to examine the concrete and possible ways that Mexican immigrant workers fit in the ethnic economy of Chicano enclaves. We have assumed that an ethnic economy is appropriate area for analyzing the impact that Mexican workers have on Chicanos. The emphasis here is on the notion that the ethnic enterprise may be as important as labor markets for explaining this impact. Thus, the focus has been on the role and function of immigrant workers in the ethnic enterprise and there is a suggestion that this relationship may bear on the over-all vitality of ethnic enclaves.

The presence of immigrant workers and their families also has many direct and indirect consequences. Many of these are positive. Some of these consequences are specific to the ethnic community and some are more important to the society at large. The following are five concluding propositions.

(1) The principal beneficiaries of the auxiliary services created by immigrant workers and their families are Chicanos and non-ethnic providers of goods and services, i.e., school teachers, policemen, lawyers, social service providers, etc. The benefits are dependent on an ethnic economy, yet oftentimes the links of this dependence are not so readily apparent and are in fact difficult to perceive.

(2) The net effect on enterprise enhancement, on job creation for direct goods and services, and on the creation of jobs through auxiliary services, may more than offset any negative effects produced in certain labor markets where immigrant workers compete with domestic workers.

(3) Immigrant workers as a source of labor may cut the cost-of-living for other ethnic residents who use their labor in informal ways, i.e., receive basic necessities or improve their standard of living by obtaining or purchasing goods or services otherwise unobtainable at prevailing costs (informal sector economic activities and exchange through labor barter).

(4) Undocumented workers subsidize society through the tax system when they contribute far more than they receive through under utilization of publicly supported service programs or benefits. Immigrant workers do not benefit in proportion to their contributions, nor do the ethnic enclaves in which they tend to live.

(5) Undocumented immigrants who work in the U.S., yet who maintain their principal place of residence and maintain households outside of the United States, provide *super-subsidies* to the tax system and to U.S. society.

Research Questions

More research is necessary in order to unravel the complexities of the impact of immigration on immigrant-receiving societies. Further research on the topic of Mexican immigration ought to take into consideration the role, function, and impact, both in historical and contemporary contexts, of this immigration on the ethnic economy. This would include developing a better understanding of the total operation of ethnic economies, the specific impact of immigration, and the importance of the informal sector in economic activity. A study of this sort ought to take into consideration the following questions.

Ethnic Economy
1. What is an ethnic economy?
2. What is the role and function of an ethnic economy?
3. What are the origins of an ethnic economy?
4. How are ethnic economies formed, expanded and contracted?
5. What means of competitive advantage do ethnic businessmen have in establishing, maintaining or expanding their businesses?
6. What are the levels of ethnic economy?

7. What maintenance and integrative functions does an ethnic economy have?
8. What are the links between an ethnic economy and its ethnic enclave?
9. How does a change in one effect a change in the other?
10. How does the composition (changing) of the population affect an ethnic economy?
11. What are the key institutions in an ethnic economy?
12. What kinds of products and services are rendered by ethnic enterprises?
13. How do ethnic enterprises branch out from an exclusively ethnic clientele to a non-ethnic clientele?
14. Does a culturally derived basis of economic organization have a role and function in ethnic economy?
15. How does entrepreneurial segregation affect the ethnic economy?
16. Do ethnic entrepreneurs enjoy "protected" commercial monopolies?
17. What businesses in the ethnic economy are peripheral to the main economy?
18. What is the entrepreneurial drive of the foreign-born?
19. What cultural and sociological factors influence ethnic concentration in restricted fields of economic endeavor?
20. How does non-ethnic competition affect an ethnic economy?
21. How does non-ethnic competition for ethnic patronage affect an ethnic economy?
22. How does minority enterprise policy affect an ethnic economy?
23. How do non-minority enterprise policies affect an ethnic economy?
24. What role can federal and state governments have in affecting a positive relationship between minority employers and immigrant workers?
25. How could a minority enterprise policy affect the socio-economic mobility of immigrant workers and their families?
26. How do international economic factors affect an ethnic economy?
27. What proportion of minority entrepreneurs are foreign-born?

Impact on Immigration
1. What is the role and function of immigrants in an ethnic economy?
2. Does a change in immigration policy affect ethnic businesses?
3. What are the similarities in the ways in which Mexican immigrants and other immigrants affect the ethnic economy? What are the dissimilarities?
4. What kinds of ethnic businesses typically hire immigrant workers?
5. Where are ethnic businesses located? What proportion of the immigrant work force is employed by ethnic businesses?
6. What proportion of the work force employed by ethnic businesses are Mexican workers?
7. How does the circulation activity of undocumented workers moving between residencies in Mexico and labor markets in the United States affect an ethnic economy?
8. Are undocumented workers a permanent feature of an ethnic economy?
9. How do the working conditions of immigrants working for ethnic employers compare to immigrants working for non-ethnic employers?
10. What are the special consumer demands made by the immigrant population?
11. How do ethnic enterprises satisfy the special consumer demands of the immigrant population?

12. How capable are ethnic enterprises of providing products and services to the immigrant population?
13. What are the possibilities for self employment among immigrant workers?

Informal Sector

1. What kinds of informal sector economic activities are in operation in the ethnic enclave?
2. How does informal sector economic activity affect the ethnic economy?
3. How do immigrants affect the informal sector?
4. What role do the foreign-born have in the informal sector?
5. How does informal sector economic activity affect the economic enclave?
6. How do international economic factors actively affect the informal sector of the ethnic economy?

Concluding Remarks

Those who believe immigrant workers have an adverse effect on the economy distort the nature of the presence of immigrant workers in the labor process. It is evident that immigrant workers are in competition for jobs with domestic workers. However, in the absence of empirical research, it is sometimes assumed that immigrant and domestic workers are necessarily in competition and that this competition has a consequently negative impact on minority communities.

As with most other policy areas, immigration has both positive and negative features that may vary according to place, sector, and industry. The question of net effect must include a variety of factors in order that a reasonable measurement may be made of this impact. Heretofore, the debate concerning immigration policy has been woefully one-sided, usually politically motivated, with an agenda determined by proponents of restrictive immigration.

These latter proponents tend to rely on the impact of immigration on minority communities. In doing so, they display a fundamental ignorance of the minority experience in the United States and they demonstrate an insensitivity to the views of minorities. Advocates of restrictive immigration justify their claims on the basis that it is in the interest of Chicanos. Obvious here is a complete lack of understanding in the ways that the Chicano community functions. More thorough research ought to reveal that the Chicano-Mexican community is not as segmented as might be expected. The Chicano-Mexicano community is the result of history, structural location, residence, family, and culture. The ethnic economy and the ethnic enclave constitute the dynamic social setting in which this organic integrative process takes place. This is particularly true in large sunbelt cities that have long maintained economically viable ethnic communities.

New immigrants do not always re-enact the experiences of earlier immigrants. The problems experienced by earlier generations of immigrants may be reproduced again, not because of their national origins, race, language, work, or cultural experience in the United States, but because of their reception by federal and state governments and the many barriers placed before them to deter and discourage their entrance to the country and their social position once they have gained admittance. These factors threaten to reproduce the long-term negative features of immigrant settlement. The elimination of unnecessary obstacles to the immigrant population benefits minorities as much as immigrants and benefits the society at large in the long run.

FOOTNOTES

1. We shall rely on the following definitions of ethnic group; By ethnic group we are referring to "a collectivity within a larger society have real or putative common ancestry, memories of a shared historical past, and a cultural focus on one or more symbolic elements defined as the epitome of their peoplehood" (R.C. Schermerhorn, 1970). "Ethnic groups are largely biologically self-perpetuating, share fundamental cultural values, realized in overt unity in cultural forms, make up a field of communication and interaction, and has a membership which identifies itself, and is identified by others, as constituting a category distinguishable from other categories of the same order" (Frederick Barth, 1969).

REFERENCES

Frederik Barth. 1969. *Ethnic Groups and Boundaries*. Boston: Little, Brown and Company.

Vernon Briggs, 1978. "Labor Market Aspects of Mexican Immigration to U.S. in the 1970's." Stanley Ross, (ed.), *Views Across the Border*, Albuquerque, New Mexico, University of New Mexico Press. pp. 204-225.

Gilbert Cardenas. 1976. "Public Data on Mexican Immigrants to U.S.: A Critical Evaluation," in W. Boyd, Littrel and Gideon Sjoberg, eds., *Current Issues in Social Policy*, Beverly Hills, California: Sage Publications, pp. 127-144.

Gilbert Cardenas, Rodolfo O. de la Garza and Niles Hansen. 1982. *Immigrants and the Ethnic Community: Mexican Immigrants and Mexican American Business*. Research proposal submitted to U.S. Department of Commerce, Solicitation No. SA-83-RSB-0013.

Joe R. Feagin. 1978. *Racial and Ethnic Relations*. Englewood Cliffs: Prentice Hall, Inc.

Ivan H. Light. 1972. *Ethnic Enterprise in America: Business and Welfare Among Chinese, Japanese, and Blacks*. Berkeley: University of California Press.

Carey McWilliams. 1948. *A Mask for Privilege: Anti-Semiticism in America*. Boston: Little Brown and Company.

Mabel Newcomer. 1961. "The little businessman: A study of business proprietors in Poughkeepsie, New York." *Business History Review* 35 (Winter, 1961).

David S. North and Miriam Houston. 1976. *The Characteristics and Role of Illegal Aliens in the U.S. Labor Market: An Exploratory Study*. Report prepared for the Employment and Training Administration, U.S. Dept. of Labor, Contract No. 20-11-74-21. Washington, D.C.: Linton and Co., Inc.

Richard A. Schermerhorn. 1970. *Comparative Ethnic Relations: A Framework for Theory and Research*. New York: Random House.

Robert Warren and Jeffrey S. Passel. 1984. "A Count of the Uncountable: Estimates of Undoc. Aliens counted in the 1980 Census." U.S. Dept. of Commerce Bureau of the Census. Unpublished paper.

CHICANO-INDOCUMENTADO WORK RELATIONS: FINDINGS OF THE TEXAS INDOCUMENTADO STUDY

Nestor Rodriguez

INTRODUCTION

Illegal Mexican immigration is a matter of social, political, and economic concern in the United States. The misconceptions concerning this migration makes it a subject of major interest for social research. Recent studies and research have contributed significantly to our understanding of *indocumentados* or undocumented Mexican immigrants. However, there are a number of areas where research is virtually non-existent. Chicano-*indocumentado* relations, particularly in the labor force, is an example of this uncharted territory.[1] This paper will attempt to describe conditions of *indocumentado* migration and settlement in the U.S., and, more specifically, it will attempt to describe relations in the labor force between Chicanos and *indocumentados*.

Just as there are misconceptions concerning the nature of illegal Mexican immigration, there are misconceptions concerning relations between Mexicans and Chicanos. Chicano leaders and intellectuals have taken an active role in the protection of rights for *indocumentados*. The plight of *indocumentados* has always been on the agenda of virtually every Chicano organization. However, one ought not to infer that there is harmony between the two groups. Depending upon the location and particular working situations, there is sometimes suspicion, tension, and competition for jobs. In view of cultural and social differences, Chicano-*indocumentado* relations present an excellent opportunity for employer exploitation. This is just one of the areas where concrete evidence is necessary in order to shape policy for Chicanos.

The description of relations between Chicanos and *indocumentados* results from an investigation of eighteen work situations in Austin, Texas. The Texas Indocumentado Study, housed at the University of Texas at Austin, was funded by a grant from the population division of the National Institute of Child Health and Human Development. Admittedly, Austin, Texas is not representative of a large industrial structure, with a large Mexican population. Austin, however, does

72

present an opportunity to generalize regarding certain aspects of Chicano-*indocumentado* relations in the workplace.

The study conducted a field investigation of the conditions of undocumented Mexican immigrants from 1980 to 1982. The metropolitan community of San Antonio nearby was used to assess the opportunity structure for the *indocumentado*, particularly in comparison to Austin. Over forty households were contacted in Austin. The focus of the information obtained concerned *indocumentado* adaptation to the Austin socio-economic environment. Special attention was placed on work conditions, dealing with public service organizations, and the education of children. The investigation methodology was ethnographic in nature. Workplace information was obtained through work site visits and through interviews with Chicanos and *indocumentados*.

The findings indicate that *indocumentados* are set apart from Chicanos. Their differentiation results from three main causes. First, employers perceive direct benefits from an isolated *indocumentado* work force. Second, the settlement pattern of *indocumentados* require endogenous survival mechanisms leading to enclave existence. Finally, because of the first and second causes above, *indocumentados* themselves, as the opportunity arises, seek to form exclusive work crews in an effort to control the labor process. The next result, as the findings point out, is the differentiation of *indocumentados* from Chicanos. The special characteristics of this differentiation are described in the findings of the eighteen work situations and in certain aspects of *indocumentado* existence in the general community.

WORKPLACE FINDINGS

The Texas Indocumentado Study in Austin investigated eighteen workplaces. The findings of this study provide for five general types of conditions in Chicano-Indocumentado relations.

(1) Work situations where Chicanos are not present.
(2) Work situations where Chicanos are present only as supervisors.
(3) Work situations where Chicanos and *indocumentados* are present in the same work place but do not share the same task.
(4) Work situations where Chicanos and *indocumentados* work in the same work place and share the same work space.
(5) Work situations where *indocumentados* supervise Chicanos.

Work situations were categorized according to a "most of the time" criterion; that is, a work situation was placed in the indicated category if the classification conditions occurred most of the time. It should be understood that the number of cases in each category is not meant to be indicative of an actual distribution. For example, only two work situations are included in the category where Chicanos are present only as supervisors. Yet, this is one of the most often observed conditions of Chicano-*indocumentado* worker relations. The intent of the workplace investigation was to define the range of work situations and not to survey the frequency of occurrence.

WORK SITUATIONS WHERE CHICANOS ARE NOT PRESENT

Of the eighteen workplaces investigated, four were found to have an absence of Chicano workers. These included a landscaping company, two Mexican restaurants, and an apartment cleaning crew. The landscaping company employed approximately fifty workers who were divided into five crews. Typical work assignments included lawn, trimming, fertilizing, and watering work, usually at office and apartment complexes. *Indocumentados* were found as crew supervisors, although they in turn were supervised by Anglos. The crews consisted of *indocumentados* who knew one another, either because they were related or because they had emigrated from the same hometown in Mexico.

In one of the two restaurants, *indocumentado* workers were also related by blood. Brothers, cousins, and two married couples were part of the fifteen member crew that did the restaurant's cooking, dishwashing, and cleaning. The remainder of the work force at this restaurant consisted of waiters, bartenders, barmaids, and managers who were Anglo. The second restaurant also had a work force consisting of Anglos and *indocumentados*, with the exception of two *arreglados*.[2] The restaurant employed thirty-five workers, of which twenty-seven were *indocumentados* who worked as kitchen workers, table cleaners, waiters, and bar help. The kitchen workers were supervised by an *indocumentado* chef from Mexico City. One of the *arreglados* was a cashier and the other, a waiter.

The apartment cleaning crew was composed of a husband and wife who were helped on occasion by two or three of their children after school. They cleaned apartments from the City of Austin Public Housing administration. Only the husband was officially contracted, through a Black supervisor, to do the cleaning work.

WORK SITUATIONS WHERE CHICANOS ARE SUPERVISORS

Two work situations were found where Chicanos were present only as supervisors. The first was a painting crew that consisted of a Chicano contractor who employed a crew of five *indocumentados*. The crew painted houses and apartments throughout the city. Their work days were among the longest encountered during the study. Usually, the Chicano contractor picked up the workers at six in the morning and brought them home at seven or eight, and sometimes nine, in the evening. While the workers felt they could endure the rigor of their typical six day workweek, they complained that the Chicano paid them $20-22 per day, which is about $1.50 per hour. They wanted the minimum wage at least. According to the *indocumentados*, they worked for the contractor only because it was the most readily available work. Two of the workers were previously employed as carpenters and the remaining three were recent first-time arrivals constrained to paying the *coyote* who brought them over.

The second work situation in this category consisted of a small welding shop owned by a Chicano. The owner would hire an *indocumentado* helper during peak periods in his business. The shop was located in a Chicano-Anglo neighborhood. The *indocumentados* were hired to prepare the materials required by the Chicano for welding. The Chicano reported that he had hired three *indocumentados* over an eighteen month period. He added that even when he did not need an assistant, he would sometimes hire *indocumentado* youths because they needed the money to survive.

WORK SITUATION WITH CHICANO-INDOCUMENTADO SEGREGATION

Five out of eighteen work situations investigated consisted of Chicanos and *indocumentados* working in different jobs in the same workplace. These included a mining plant, a cement company, a car dealership, a tortilla factory, and a bridge construction site. The hierarchy of the mining plant consisted of Anglo managers, Chicano and Anglo foremen, Chicano and Anglo truck drivers and heavy machinery operators, and *indocumentado* laborers. The number of *indocumentado* employees varied from eighty to one hundred, depending on the volume of business. Their work was mainly bagging minerals and loading boxcars. At times, they also handled very hot ovens used to purify extracted materials. Chicanos and Anglos handled the conveyor equipment that brought the raw materials into the plant for purification and bagging. During peak business periods, the plant operated in three eight-hour shifts. Among *indocumentado* complaints were the heat from the ovens in summer, alkaline burns, and a Chicano supervisor who drove them too hard. Here, too, many of the *indocumentados* were related and their workplace socializing was limited to themselves.

The cement company was a branch of a national corporation that manufactures cement structures for commercial, industrial and highway construction. The workplace hierarchy is organized as in the mining plant. Top management is Anglo, work supervisors are Anglo and Chicano, skilled work (welding and other iron work) and machine operating is done by Anglos and some Chicanos. The unskilled laborers are almost all *indocumentados*. Approximately one half of the work force, totaling one hundred, is *indocumentado*. Their work schedules depend upon the level of business.

Under the supervision of Chicanos, the *indocumentados* prepare materials for cement casting, and guide the transporting of the multi-ton structures to the storage areas. The *indocumentados* consider this latter duty to be very dangerous. A structure, for example, could fall and crush everything and everyone under it. During loading, a cable could break and the structure could swing wildly, injuring anyone in the way. Though the *indocumentados* have contact with other workers in the company, the majority of their interaction is among themselves as members of the manufacturing and transporting crews. Several of the *indocumentados* are related by blood and many are from the same hometown in Mexico.

The tortilla factory employed thirteen *indocumentados*, eleven women and two men. The factory was Chicano-owned and it was located in the old Mexican section of Austin. The store itself was important for *indocumentados* because they could buy traditional food items which were not available at other stores. The female *indocumentados* worked mainly in packing corn and flour tortillas and other corn products by machine. Their work situation was a large table next to a tortilla producing machine. The two male *indocumentados* fed ingredients in the machine and stocked packaged items. Three Chicanos made truck deliveries to stores and a Chicana took care of the cash register. The owner supervised all of the work at a pace set by the machine. Most of the employee socializing occurred at the packaging table. The women chatted as they kept pace with the machine, the Chicanos were usually making deliveries, and the Chicana was kept busy with customers in the front of the store.

In the bridge construction site, twelve *indocumentados* were employed as laborers to assist iron and other skilled workers in preparing materials and in operating machines. The *indocumentados* in this work situation were employed by a company located in El Paso, Texas. This company was responsible for the iron and cement work on the bridge. Their work duties ranged from unloading trailers in small crews to doing cement finishing, to assisting the Chicano iron workers.

The car dealership employed *indocumentados* in the *make ready department*. The six-man *indocumentado* crew was supervised by an Anglo. They were responsible for washing and waxing newly sold cars. The *indocumentado* crew was separated from the rest of the service department, which included Chicanos, by a wall. The workers in the crew were close friends. Five of them were from the state of Michoacan and shared living quarters.

WORK SITUATIONS WITH CHICANO-INDOCUMENTADO CO-WORKERS

Chicanos and *indocumentados* shared the same workplace and work space in a college dormitory, a commercial laundry, a mattress factory, a cafeteria, a barrios restaurant, and a motel. The service staff in the dormitory complex, housing approximately three hundred and forty students in three dormitories, consisted of fifty-one Anglos, Chicanos, Blacks, and *indocumentados*. Under a Chicano supervisor, the *indocumentados*, six males and two females, worked as part of the kitchen staff along with Chicanos and Blacks. The *indocumentados*, which included three family members, did cooking, dishwashing and food serving tasks. There was considerable interaction between the Chicano supervisor and the *indocumentados*, particularly after work. For example, he helped one of the *indocumentados* enroll in an English class and accompanied them when they made expensive purchases, such as stereos and televisions.

The commercial cleaners is part of a chain of laundries in the city of Austin. They clean uniforms, sheets, and other textile item for businesses in the city. Its fifty-member work force consists of Anglos, Chicanos, *indocumentados*, and a few Asians. Male and female *indocumentados* are in a majority of twenty-five or so laundry room workers. Their supervisor is an Anglo. As in the tortilla factory, the work pace is set by machines, dryers, and ironing equipment. The pace of work is quite fast and there is very little opportunity for interaction. Male *indocumentados* operate the large washers. Female *indocumentadas* fold sheets and other items that come from the dryers. This is uncomfortable work as the women sometimes burn their fingers as they fold the items. The work pace is so fast here that the women will label "damaged" on sheets in order to throw them away and keep pace with the dryers. During their lunch break, the *indocumentados* eat among themselves in small groups. Some of them are related or are from the same hometown.

In the mattress factory, approximately thirty *indocumentados*, male and female, worked with about forty Chicanos and Blacks on the assembly line. The factory had a history of unsuccessful unionization attempts. It maintained a rigid work schedule supervised by Anglos and a Native American. The workers had the incentive to earn pay bonuses if they maintained a rapid work pace. The only opportunity for interaction came during lunch when workers shared tables in the lunch room. Most of the *indocumentados* ate together given that several were blood relatives or were close friends. Occasionally, Chicanos and *indocumentados* ate at the same table.

Male and female *indocumentados* worked with Anglos, Chicanos, and Blacks in the cafeteria. Of the eleven *indocumentados* in the thirty member work force, three males worked in the kitchen area, two females worked in the serving line, and six females worked as cleaners and servers in the dining room area. The female *indocumentadas* spoke with each other in Spanish, while the Anglo, Black, and Chicano cleaners and servers spoke with each other in English. This pattern of socializing carried over into the lunch break. Some of the female *indocumentadas* brought their own lunches. The *indocumentados* sat and ate together in small groups. Some of the female *indocumentadas* were related and several shared living quarters.

Two female *indocumentadas* worked in the restaurant located in the barrio. Their co-workers included six Chicano cooks, waitresses, and dishwashers. One of the women worked as a cook and the other, a fifteen year-old, worked as a table cleaner and later as a waitress. There was constant interaction between the two women and the Chicano workers. When the table cleaner was promoted to the position of waitress, the Chicano owners made her study the menu and practice taking orders in English.

Chicanos and *indocumentados* also worked in similar jobs at the motel. Under the supervision of a female Puerto Rican, female *indocumentados* and four Chicanas cleaned rooms. *Indocumentados* also worked in maintenance, groundskeeping, and in the laundry. There was little interaction between the *indocumentados* and the Chicanas who worked as maids. They were assigned to different wings of the motel. Several of the *indocumentados* were related and lived together.

WORK SITUATIONS WITH INDOCUMENTADO SUPERVISORS AND CHICANO WORKERS

The study found only one work situation where an *indocumentado* had work authority over Chicanos. This work situation was a wall mortaring and plastering crew with a Chicano supervisor, four *indocumentados*, and four Chicanos. The crew was part of a company based in El Paso, Texas and they traveled through the state working in apartment construction sites. The *indocumentados* were skilled workers and the Chicanos were helpers. When the Chicano supervisor of this crew took a temporary leave to inspect a prospective work site, two of the *indocumentados* were placed in charge of the crew. On other occasions, one of the more experienced *indocumentados* would be sent to supervise crews working in other cities.

This work crew was unique. While the majority of the workers in the study were paid the minimum wage or less, the *indocumentados* in this work crew were paid an average of $6.50 an hour. Lodging was provided for them in motels at company expense. The crew was also unique in cohesiveness. There was constant joking at work and in the evening it was common for all the workers to socialize together. The *indocumentados* in this case exhibited social characteristics different from those of other workers in the study. For example, they traveled by air on their trips to Mexico and back. They dressed fashionably and for entertainment chose establishments catering to a business clientele.

These workplace findings indicate that Chicano-*indocumentado* relations in Austin may be characterized by differentiation. In two instances, Chicanos are completely absent from the workplace of *indocumentados*, in others they are present only as supervisors. When Chicanos and *indocumentados* share the same workplace and work space, they tend to be separated socially even though they may perform similar tasks. The social division is evidenced by their separation into isolated groups either in the work space or during lunch breaks. The findings indicate an absence of social division in only two cases, the barrio restaurant and the plastering crew. While no definitive claim can be made, the proportion of cases in each of the categories is representative of Austin, and the range of categories indicates that differentiation between Chicano and *indocumentados* is a significant factor in Chicano-*indocumentado* relations in Austin.

INTERPRETATION OF FINDINGS

The finding of differentiation in Chicano-*indocumentado* work relations illustrates a prevalent condition of labor forces in modern capitalist societies. Historically, it has been in the interest of the capitalist class to increase their economic power by creating divisions in the labor force. These divisions are commonly created by hiring workers of different races, ethnic groups, and religions (Edwards, Reich, and Gordon, 1975). This strategy is useful in that employers reduce the possibility of worker solidarity, hence opposition, and thus they increase the opportunity for profits. The use of immigrant workers in modern labor history has been instrumental in maintaining labor force division. First, an immigrant is alienated from the native-born workers. Second, in the case of questionable entry, the immigrant worker has only a tenuous residency status and is thus susceptible to employer manipulation. In some instances, immigrant workers constitute the total work force of a work situation, and in others, they form only a part. As shall be determined, however, labor segmentation is not always a conscious strategy on the part of an employer. *Indocumentados* can and do contribute to labor segregation by their own actions. This can occur as a consequence of their settlement survival strategies and as a consequence of trying to improve poor working conditions by forming homogeneous work groups in the workplace.

EMPLOYER STRATEGY

It is evident that some employers, and this group includes Chicanos, prefer to hire *indocumentados*. A Chicano employer in San Antonio gives the following reasons:

> The workers from here (Chicanos) do not want to work. They do not know how to work. They just come one day, and the next day they will not come . . . *Los mojaditos* are good workers. They work at any time. That is why we use them. They come to work and to make money. No, they are not like the workers from here . . . I want good workers. Good workers that just want to work.

A persistent view held by employers suggests that *indocumentados* are willing to work harder than Chicanos. This was common throughout the study. Sometimes an employer would add that Chicano workers have been spoiled by welfare programs and food stamps. For employers, the designation of *indocumentados* as good workers means more than simply producing more on the job. Among other benefits that employers obtain from good *indocumentado* workers are the following:[3]

1. *Flexible work schedules.* The Austin work sites in the study had very flexible work schedules. Sometimes, the *indocumentados* worked well over forty

hours per week and sometimes considerably less. For example, during a lull in business activity at the cement company, *indocumentados* worked one or two days a week. When business picked up, the work schedule might extend to ten hours a day, six days per week. In the landscaping company, *indocumentados* sometimes worked seven days straight with no overtime compensation for new workers. In the painting crew, the work might stretch from fifteen hours in length, with the workers permitted to eat only when traveling between work sites.

For employers, the two chief benefits to be derived from a flexible work schedule are not paying a worker for an eight-hour day when there is little or no work to be done and the ability to increase considerably the number of hours worked per day without a commensurate increase in compensation to the employee.

2. *Recruitment of workers.* The study also revealed that employers relied on the *indocumentados* to recruit other *indocumentados* when additional workers were needed. This created what amounts to a reserve labor pool. *Indocumentados*, it seems, always had a relative, brother, sister, etc., who needed work, wanted to change jobs, or was coming from Mexico. To some extent, this method of recruitment created an exclusive labor market for *indocumentados*. It is likely as well that the closed employment atmosphere precluded itinerant workers from applying for work in such places.

3. *Savings on Safety.* Employers of *indocumentados* were spared the expense of providing an occupational safe environment for the workers. For example, the mining plant did not provide protective gear for the *indocumentados* working with the hot ovens, nor were any protective measures available to prevent alkaline burns. During the summer heat, removal of shirts was the only comfort available in the presence of so much heat. After work, they cleaned chemical substances from their bodies by means of an air hose. *Indocumentados* in the cement plant had the protection of hard hats, but not steel-toe boots or heavy gloves. As a result, the workers suffered broken toes and sheared fingers.

4. *Precluding union organizing.* Work situations with a relatively small number of employees, such as paint crew, would not be targeted by unionization efforts. The same is not true of the mattress factory and cement company. The mattress factors is adjacent to another mattress factory which experienced intensive labor organizing in the recent past. The cement company was the object of organizing efforts during the period of the study. Union officials set up an information table at a location frequented by the workers during lunch. Almost all of the workers shunned the table. Many of the workers did not read or write and thus could not read the notices or sign their names to contact lists. These factors relative to the *indocumentados* are clearly advantageous to employers.

Some employers, no doubt, also receive such advantages from U.S. workers, however, *indocumentados* are particularly vulnerable. Their illegal status and their lack of familiarity with government work regulations or worker compensation laws make them especially attractive for employers. One *indocumentado*, for example, who worked for two weeks clearing brush without being paid was afraid to complain for fear that the employer would report his relatives to the Immigration and Naturalization Service. In the cement company, according to some *indocumentados*, workers injured on the job were dismissed by the company without any compensation at all.

In some cases, employers contribute to Chicano-*indocumentado* segregation by hiring homogeneous *indocumentado* work crews. Some employers contribute to segregation tension by insisting to the *indocumentados* that Chicanos are inferior workers. Several times during interviews, *indocumentados* quoted their employers as the source for their contention that "los chicanos son muy flojos" (Chicanos are very lazy).

It is not always clear where the preference for undocumented workers originates. This is particularly true of large workplaces. In the mining company, management clearly included *indocumentados* in planning their work force. Many of the workers lived in company shacks located near the plant and used the company store for grocery, money-order and postal services. In fact, according to one worker, the company has depended upon Mexican migrant labor since the turn of the century. The source of *indocumentado* preference in the cement company was not as clear. For the two-year duration of the study, all of the company's laborers were *indocumentados*. In late 1982, however, one of the foremen assembled an Anglo and Black crew. Some of the *indocumentados* believed that the Chicano foreman did not like "mojados."

Endogenous Social Network

The segregation between Chicano and *indocumentado* workers is also an outgrowth of the social life of *indocumentados* in the United States. It is an existence with many of the characteristics of an enclave. When *indocumentados* migrate they do not integrate themselves into the Chicano working-class *barrios*. Instead, *indocumentado* arrivals tend to settle in neighborhoods with many *indocumentado* residents. Upon arrival, many of them become members of existing *indocumentado* households. In this way, the recent *indocumentado* becomes part of a social structure which includes scattered *indocumentado* households in the city and, most importantly, which extends to the workplace. Within this social structure, the *indocumentado* has available a number of resources (social, cultural, and economic) upon which to draw for housing, food, recreation, transportation, and work.[4] The recently-arrived *indocumentado* is limited almost entirely to this social structure.

Ethnic solidarity and the desire to be with one's own is no doubt a significant element in the creation, maintenance, and growth of *indocumentado* enclaves, but other factors are also important. Endogenous networks enable *indocumentados* to maintain a relative autonomy in their migration. This is true despite the stress of illegal entry. This is in contrast to those periods when Mexican labor was imported by governmental design. Carefully circumscribed internal networks are crucial to this autonomy. In Austin, for example, the *indocumentado* enclave provides for *coyotes*, information, and cash assistance for an immigrant to journey to the United States. It would not be uncommon for an *indocumentado* within the enclave to raise as much as $2,000.00 in cash in one or two days in order to bring over a family. The same holds true for certain cash emergencies where the *indocumentado* does not have the financial and credit resources available to certain U.S. workers.

The endogenous social structure of the *indocumentado* may also be seen as a consequence of a wider social context. *Indocumentados* are generally limited to low-paying jobs. Because of their questionable status, they and their families are excluded from public assistance programs. Multiple-family or contiguous households reduce living expenses. Two families living together can share rent and food expenses. Taking in relatives or co-workers as boarders insures the *indocumentado's* ability to pay the rent in the event he is out of work.

The denial of public assistance resources to *indocumentados* may serve perhaps, to reinforce their differentiation from Chicanos. As *indocumentados* are forced to rely almost exclusively upon their own social structures for support, the opportunity for social interaction with Chicanos is lessened, if not entirely precluded. The social aspects of Chicano-*indocumentado* differentiation are similarly present in workplace relations. *Indocumentados* tended to be isolated from Chicanos in all but one of the workplaces studied. In the *barrio* restaurant, and perhaps this is a key to the differentiation, the *undocumented* women worked among a greater number of Chicano workers. Also, neither was treated as "*indocumentado* labor" by the employer.

Controlling the Labor Process

The findings in the two Mexican restaurants with all-*indocumentado* kitchen crews indicate a third important factor which may lead to Chicano-*indocumentado* work differentiation. In both of the restaurants, the *indocumentado* chefs replaced Chicano kitchen help with *indocumentado* workers. The reason for the shift in laborers is to strengthen control of the labor process. This sort of activity is not unusual nor is it peculiar to the *indocumentados*. It is quite common in the American workplace. Research in labor relations abounds with evidence to support the notion that workers tend to shape the process of production and to structure the social aspects of work for their own benefit. Marx contended that relations of production create their own logic and that worker control is an integral part of it.

The struggle for dominance as a characteristic of *indocumentado* labor relations may be difficult to accept. This is a direct challenge to stereotypical perceptions. *Indocumentados* cannot be classified as "anarcho-syndicalists," but neither are they "submissive fatalists" when it comes to workplace relations in class struggles.

The work resistance tactics of *indocumentados* mirror those of other workers. The response to abusive and demanding employers is a change of jobs.[5] Prolonging a task may delay or prevent reassignment to another more arduous one. Denying knowledge of how to operate machinery or equipment prevents being shifted to different tasks throughout the workday. Pretending not to understand instructions given in English delays assignment to a task until a translator, usually a Chicano, arrives. Work resistance tactics tend to vary according to the *indocumentados'* length of stay in the United States. Recent arrivals tend to be more assertive on the job than *indocumentados* who have been in the country for some time and who know "como trabajan las cosas aqui" (how things are done here).

Individual work resistance tactics do not affect Chicano-*indocumentado* segregation. Segregation, however, is affected by social strategies to gain control of the labor process. The two *indocumentado* chefs argue that the replacement of Chicanos in the kitchen crew with *indocumentados* enables the crew to work more effectively. One of the chefs described the process:

> In the kitchen everyone is given a station. They have to make the food between two and five-thirty in the evening, when we start serving the orders and everyone has to be ready with the work. And right now, we try to hire only *camaradas* so it can be done. Because we are in a situation where we know each other, when one is not able to finish the work, the other will help. And that way no worker will be scolded, because we are united. When we are different everyone just wants to finish his or her work. And the worker has to make it however he

or she can. That is the way it is if we do not know each other, if we are not from the same state, from the same land, even if we are from Mexico. We the Mexicans, have got to get along well together.

Once in place, the *indocumentado* crew informally reorganized the kitchen work so that the previous occupational structure of the restaurants was changed. Once the crew was completely *indocumentado*, the work became a collective effort even though each worker was still officially assigned to a specific task. With the workplace informally reorganized as a collective, the workers themselves decided who could be absent and who worked which shift. This collective work situation did not exist while Chicanos were part of the kitchen crew.

It is not always necessary to remove Chicanos from the workplace in order to gain control of the labor process. The development of a homogeneous *indocumentado* crew is simply a matter of not hiring Chicanos, or if one is hired, to isolate him. For example, in the automobile dealership, *indocumentados* in the "make ready" department were vociferously opposed to Chicanos. When a Chicano was hired in the department, the *indocumentados* left him completely alone. After a few days, following an incident with the manager, the Chicano was dismissed.

This second method used by *indocumentados* to develop a homogeneous work crew is probably the most common in all work situations. As the findings of the study indicate, *indocumentados* rarely have the authority to make personnel decisions. This *indocumentado* strategy of work control has a dialectical effect on Chicano-indocumentado work differentiation. In the short run, the strategy of developing work forces completely of *indocumentados* contributes to the separation between Chicano and *indocumentado* workers. In the long run, however, homogeneous work crews become a source of solidarity among *indocumentados* and, thus, lessen the difference in worker-power between these two groups.

CONCLUSION

The differentiated aspects of Chicano-*indocumentado* relations, as suggested by the findings of the study, will likely continue so long as the basic conditions of their labor relations remain unchanged. The three basic conditions of isolation, endogeny, and dominance, constitute the framework of a system which is difficult to change. It is in the interest of employers to perpetuate the system as it is. Social and cultural differences between Chicanos and *indocumentados* favor employers who, wittingly or unwittingly, create isolated and alienated work crews. Low pay and virtually no access to public assistance resources, which would be exacerbated by the proposed Simpson-Mazzoli legislation, will force *indocumentados* to rely on themselves for survival and this in turn will solidify their enclave existence. The impetus for *indocumentado* dominance in the labor process will continue to be a significant factor in view of the two basic conditions above. This current situation is likely to continue until the children of this generation of Chicanos and *indocumentados* enter the labor force. At that point, the children of *indocumentados* will be more knowledgeable about U.S. society, especially the English language.

There is another possibility for reducing the differentiated aspects of Chicano-*indocumentado* relations. Because the social conditions which exist in Austin are atypical in terms of Mexican immigration and in terms of Chicano-*indocumentado* relations, the example of San Antonio may be instructive. San

Antonio is a traditional destination for Mexican immigrants. Isolation between both groups is relatively less than it is in other urban centers and hence there is a greater integration of the immigrant into the Chicano community. This being the case, there is a greater likelihood that the mutual acceptance of Chicanos and *indocumentados* carries over into the workplace. Yet, one must be cautious of the social structure of San Antonio. Chicanos are a majority in the city's population and the city is capable of absorbing Mexican immigration without major disruptions in Chicano-*indocumentado* relations. The stability of these relations could suffer if, for example, there were a rapid rise in Mexican immigration to the point where they could not be readily absorbed into the labor force. This could result in increased tension between the two groups and it would force the *indocumentados* to adopt the strategies revealed in the Austin study as a matter of survival.

This is a lesson in the assertiveness of *indocumentados* for the student of labor segmentation. Just as employers will use segmented work forces to improve their profits, so can immigrants use the same structures to improve their working conditions. By limiting themselves to certain jobs and by promoting the development of exclusive work crews, *indocumentados* create the conditions necessary to control the labor process and in turn to improve their work conditions. As the two cases in Austin demonstrated, the possibility exists that *indocumentados*, who now collectively perform certain tasks, will collectively demand work improvements from employers. The prevention of such solidarity is the reason employers attempt to segment their labor force.

I am thankful to Julia Curry, Rogelio Nunez, and Harriet Romo for their helpful comments.

FOOTNOTES

1. For extensive bibliographies of works concerning undocumented Mexican immigration see Cornelius (1978) and Cornelius et al. (1982). Esteven Flores' (1982) study of the Chicano-indocumentado interface is a notable exception to the failure of works to address the topic of Chicano-*indocumentado* relations.
2. *"Arreglados"* ("arranged") is the term used by *indocumentados* to refer to fellow immigrants that have legalized their status.
3. Here I describe only economic benefits in the workplace. For discussions concerning general political benefits that employers derive from foreign workers, see Gorz (1970) and Castells (1975).
4. One *indocumentado* arrived in Austin, from the southern state of Mexico, at five-thirty in the morning, and an hour and a half later, at seven, he was already at work in a construction site with his cousin, also an *indocumentado*.
5. This is an old tactic of immigrant workers, and perhaps the most frequently practiced. Erickson (1977) describes the use of this tactic by English and Scottish immigrants in the nineteenth century.

REFERENCES

Castells, Manual. 1975. "Immigrant Workers and Class Struggle in Advanced Capitalism: The Western European Experience." *Politics and Society* 5 (1):33-36.

Cornelius, Wayne A. 1978. "Mexican Migration To The United States: Causes, Consequences, and U.S. Responses." Paper presented to the Study Group on Immigration and U.S. Foreign Policy, Council on Foreign Relations, Washington, D.C., June 8, 1978. Migration and Development Study Group, Center for International Studies, Massachusetts Institute of Technology.

Cornelius, Wayne A., Leo R. Chavez, and Jorge G. Castro. 1982. *Mexican Immigrants and Southern California: A Summary of Current Knowledge*. Research Report Series 36. Center for U.S.-Mexican Studies. University of California, San Diego.

Edwards, Richard C., Michael Reich, and David M. Gordon (eds.). 1975. *Labor Market Segmentation*. Lexington, Massachusetts: Lexington Books.

Erickson, Charlotte. 1972. *Invisible Immigrants: The adaptation of English and Scottish immigrants in 19th century America*. Coral Gables, Florida: University of Miami Press.

Flores, Estevan. 1982. "Post-Bracero Undocumented Mexican Immigration to the United States and Political Recomposition." Ph.D. dissertation, The University of Texas at Austin.

Gorz, Andre. 1970. "Immigrant Labour." *New Left Review* 61 (May-June):28-31.